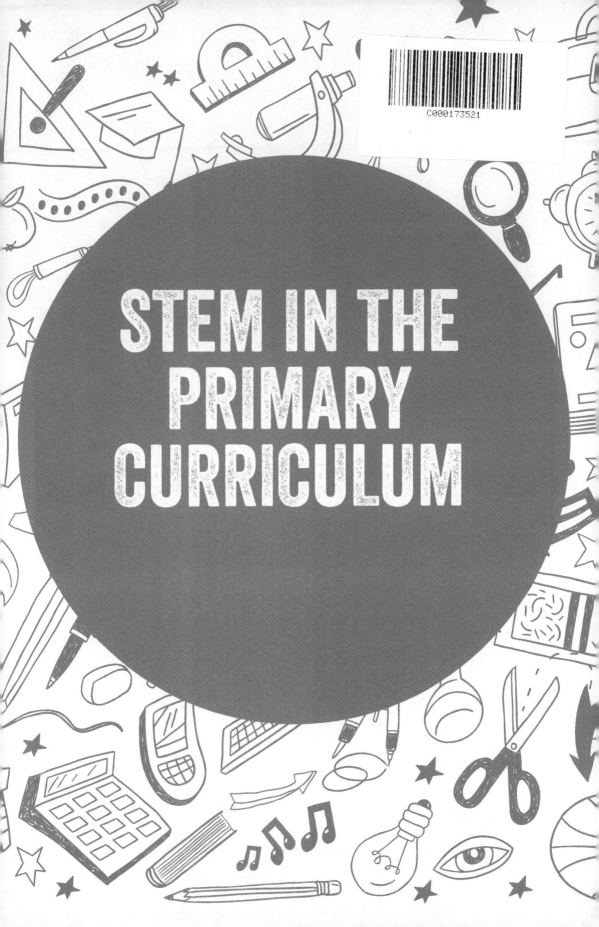

STEM IN THE PRIMARY CURRICULUM

Sara Miller McCune founded SAGE Publishing in 1965 to support the dissemination of usable knowledge and educate a global community. SAGE publishes more than 1000 journals and over 800 new books each year, spanning a wide range of subject areas. Our growing selection of library products includes archives, data, case studies and video. SAGE remains majority owned by our founder and after her lifetime will become owned by a charitable trust that secures the company's continued independence.

Los Angeles | London | New Delhi | Singapore | Washington DC | Melbourne

STEM IN THE PRIMARY CURRICULUM

EDITED BY
HELEN CALDWELL
SUE POPE

$SAGE | Learning Matters

Learning Matters
An imprint of SAGE Publications Ltd
1 Oliver's Yard
55 City Road
London EC1Y 1SP

SAGE Publications Inc.
2455 Teller Road
Thousand Oaks, California 91320

SAGE Publications India Pvt Ltd
B 1/I 1 Mohan Cooperative Industrial Area
Mathura Road
New Delhi 110 044

SAGE Publications Asia-Pacific Pte Ltd
3 Church Street
#10-04 Samsung Hub
Singapore 049483

Editor: Amy Thornton
Senior project editor: Chris Marke
Project management: Swales & Willis Ltd,
    Exeter, Devon
Marketing manager: Lorna Patkai
Cover design: Wendy Scott
Typeset by: C&M Digitals (P) Ltd, Chennai, India
Printed in the UK

Library of Congress Control Number: 2018965494

British Library Cataloguing in Publication Data

A catalogue record for this book is available from the
British Library

ISBN 978-1-5264-7436-0
ISBN 978-1-5264-7435-3 (pbk)

At SAGE we take sustainability seriously. Most of our products are printed in the UK using responsibly sourced
papers and boards. When we print overseas we ensure sustainable papers are used as measured by the
PREPS grading system. We undertake an annual audit to monitor our sustainability.

CONTENTS

ABOUT THE EDITORS AND CONTRIBUTORS

THE EDITORS

Helen Caldwell is a Senior Lecturer at the University of Northampton, where she is curriculum lead for primary computing in Teacher Education and programme lead for the Postgraduate Certificate in Digital Leadership. Her teaching covers the use of technology across primary subjects, implementing the computing curriculum and assistive technologies for SEND. Helen was a member of the Computing in ITE Expert Group and currently sits on the Technology, Pedagogy and Education Association (TPEA) National Executive Committee. Her research interests include social online learning in higher education, and computing and digital literacy in primary education.

Sue Pope was Associate Head of the School of Teacher Education and Professional Development at Manchester Metropolitan University. For five years, she was the national lead for mathematics 5–19 at the Qualifications and Curriculum Authority (QCA), with responsibility for STEM. She moved to QCA after ten years in higher education working with beginning and practising teachers. She worked as a local authority adviser after teaching for ten years in a number of schools. Sue is a long-standing active member of the Association of Teachers of Mathematics.

THE CONTRIBUTORS

Yasemin Allsop worked as an ICT Coordinator and a class teacher in primary schools in London for almost ten years. She currently works as a Lecturer in Primary Education at the Institute of Education, University College London. She leads and teaches Master's level computing modules for ITE students on PGCE and SCITT programmes. Her research focus is children's thinking, learning and metacognition when making computer games. Additionally, she is interested in developing approaches for teachers to use when assessing children's computational thinking activities. She is the co-editor of the *International Journal of Computer Science Education in Schools* (www.ijcses.org).

David Barlex is an acknowledged leader in design and technology education, curriculum design and curriculum materials development. He taught in comprehensive schools for fifteen years before taking university positions in teacher education. He directed the Nuffield Design & Technology Project and was Educational Manager for Young Foresight. David is well known for his interest and expertise in developing curriculum materials that support learning from a constructivist perspective. He uses this approach to develop young people's ability to understand and critique the design decisions made by professional designers and those they make themselves in design and technology lessons.

Mick Chesterman is a lead on the delivery of the Man Met's EdLab Units. The focus of EdLab is to bridge gaps between university and community partners by co-creating innovative programmes of education. Mick's background in teaching is wide, involving over twenty years of community based education, languages, and community-based technology. Since the beginning of the Web, he has been an advocate of using technology in an appropriate way to help the aims of community and campaign groups. Much of his work has been about creating accessible learning resources for tech tools culminating in the coordination the FLOSS Manuals project, promoting Free Manuals for Free Software.

Jean Edwards is a Senior Lecturer in the Faculty of Education and Humanities at the University of Northampton. Before this she was a teacher, deputy head and headteacher in primary schools in Northamptonshire and Bedfordshire. Her specialist subjects are English, art and using digital technology in learning.

Sway Grantham is a Computing Teacher at Giffard Park Primary School and a Digital Technology Consultant. Being a Specialist Leader in Education for Primary Computing and ICT in Milton Keynes, Sway gets to work with a range of teachers on many exciting projects. She was invited as a 'lead learner' to attend the first ever Raspberry Picademy, becoming a Raspberry Pi Certified Teacher, and she loves the opportunities these cheap computers offer. She has also successfully completed the Google Innovator Academy and has been a Google Coach and Mentor meeting educators around the world and sharing their goals for improving education on a global level. She promotes the importance of using technology as a tool across the curriculum and loves inspiring children and adults through digital making and STEM-based activities.

Anne Guilford was a Senior Lecturer within the Faculty of Education at Manchester Metropolitan University for nine years until summer 2018. She now works ad hoc for the university. Prior to this Anne taught Design and Technology for thirty years in secondary schools including a year as an adviser for all key stages in design and technology. Her specialist subjects are textiles and food.

Eleanor Hoskins is a Senior Lecturer in the Faculty of Education at Manchester Metropolitan University. Prior to this, she taught for ten years in several primary and early years settings across two different LAs and gained experience as science and numeracy subject leaders as well as taking responsibility for assessment and SENCo. In addition, she was a School Improvement Teacher for Manchester LA, Assistant Head and Deputy Headteacher. In school, she contributed to the creation and organisation of a new open plan Foundation stage before it became popular in other schools and settings. She trialled new approaches to continuous provision learning and transition from EYFS to KS1. Her research interests lie in the field of early years science exploration and technology, the focus of her Master's dissertation and recent publications.

Sarah Lister is a Senior Lecturer at Manchester Metropolitan University, co-ordinating the modern foreign languages provision within the initial primary teacher education programmes. Her research and academic enterprise include motivation, early language learning, using technology in the language classroom and CLIL. She first became interested and involved in CLIL in 2008. She led a European CLIL project *Linked Up* from 2010 to 2012. She worked with Pauline Palmer on a Knowledge Transfer partnership (KTP) project between the Manchester Met and a commercial software company, Cyber Coach (2016–2018) to develop a series of innovative, cutting-edge game-based learning resources aimed at supporting language learning and mathematics. They recently secured funding from the EU to work with several European partners on an Erasmus Plus project to investigate using a game-based approach to teaching curriculum subjects through a second language.

Rania Maklad joined Manchester Metropolitan University in 2011, and has been the Primary Science Subject Lead since 2015. She contributes to the undergraduate and postgraduate teaching programmes in primary science. Rania is also the School-based Training Lead for the final-year undergraduate programme. Her research interests include primary science, multilingualism and initial teacher education. Prior to joining the university, she taught primary aged children in Scotland and Egypt for 15 years.

Pauline Palmer teaches on the undergraduate and postgraduate initial teacher education programmes at Manchester Metropolitan University and the STEM Master's programme. Her research interests include change management and mathematics pedagogy. Always interested in the use of talk in the mathematics classroom, she has been examining CLIL pedagogy since 2013, which led to collaboration with Sarah Lister. They are keen to explore the synergies between mathematics and MFL (Modern Foreign Languages) and how CLIL can be used as an effective pedagogical tool to enhance linguistic and cognitive development in both mathematics and MFL.

Rebecca Patterson is a Senior Lecturer in Drama Education at Manchester Metropolitan University where she has worked since 2005. She is subject coordinator for Secondary PGCE Drama. Rebecca began her career working in theatre in education before studying for an LLB and then returning to Drama as a high school teacher. She has an MA in Performance Practice and is a Doctor of Education. She has a particular interest in the development of a curriculum that is accessible to all.

Alison Ramsay taught Drama and Theatre Studies for fifteen years in a large secondary school in Bolton. She left the school in 2011 to undertake an MA in Applied Theatre at the University of Manchester, where her research interests included girls and drama education, and how drama in the contemporary classroom is measured and valued. She is currently employed as a tutor in the Faculty of Education at Manchester Metropolitan University, where she is also studying for her Doctorate in Education.

Ben Sedman is a Senior Lecturer in the Faculty of Education at Manchester Metropolitan University. Previous to this role he taught for seven years in the primary sector. Ben currently teaches in the STEM Division at MMU, delivering primary Design and Technology and computing sessions to beginning and practising teachers. He has completed his MA in Education, has been involved in a European funded project and helps coordinate the Erasmus Exchange Programme. Ben is interested in a range of creative teaching approaches and enjoys photography. Some of his work can be viewed at www.bensedmanphotography.com.

Amanda Smith is a Principal Lecturer at Manchester Metropolitan University. Her background is in secondary school teaching, where she held responsibility as Head of Science and developed and delivered a range of innovative CPD and resources based in original research through her LEA and local school clusters. She worked closely with Manchester Metropolitan University developing secondary science mentoring processes for ITE students. On leaving school teaching in 2003, Amanda took up an academic role as Director of the Science Learning Centre North West, a centre of excellence for science CPD for teachers, technicians and teaching assistants, funded by the DCSF and Wellcome Trust. Currently she leads 'STEM Education Manchester' at Manchester Metropolitan University. Amanda is an active member of the North West ASE committee and ASE futures group.

Neil Smith is a Senior Lecturer in the School of Computing and Communications at the Open University. His interests are artificial intelligence, data science, machine learning, digital making, and the pedagogy of computing. He has particular interest in widening participation in computing and STEAM subjects, including children in schools and participants of all ages in informal settings. He runs a Code Club in a local primary school and has run and participated in many outreach events, such as Girls Code MK, Raspberry Pi Jams, and Cryptoparties.

INTRODUCTION: WHAT IS STEM EDUCATION?

SUE POPE

The term STEM is used to describe science, technology, engineering and mathematics, and related disciplines and applications. In school, science, mathematics, computing, and design and technology (D&T) are distinct subjects, and engineering rarely features. In the workplace, science, technology, engineering and mathematics are used together to solve practical challenges and enable modern society to operate. From the infrastructure of our homes and society (energy, water, telecommunications, travel, etc.) to the design of cities, buildings, vehicles and technical equipment (clothing, washing machines, food), STEM experts work together to meet the needs and aspirations of modern society. STEM education is concerned with raising awareness of the importance and relevance of STEM in our everyday lives and the role of individuals within STEM.

The purpose of STEM education is to develop STEM literacy - an ability to engage with understanding in modern debates about scientific and technological developments and their implications. In our modern highly interconnected global society, STEM literacy is essential for full participation and responsible citizenship. As described in the Royal Society's Vision Report (Royal Society, 2014, p. 26):

> People who think scientifically and mathematically are able to apply particular types of thinking (e.g. logical or critical thinking) learned in the classroom or the laboratory to the world beyond. This can help them to make informed judgements about contemporary scientific issues (such as how best to control TB in cattle) or decisions, for instance on medical treatments, based on an analysis of the risks. Over and above teaching the disciplines themselves, science and mathematics education in schools and colleges should show how these subjects contribute to the creation of wealth and the nation's good health. It should also demonstrate how science and technology pose threats to society and the importance of making choices informed by an understanding of risk and ethics.

STEM education is a means of offering coherent learning experiences that make connections between the individual curriculum subjects explicit and enhances learning in all of them. A STEM approach puts children at the centre of learning, helping them to use and develop skills across the curriculum in meaningful ways.

Since 1976, when James Callaghan made his famous Ruskin College speech, education has been positioned as vital to securing a successful economy. While education is much more than simply preparing the future workforce, it is important that young people are well prepared to secure their own economic wellbeing, which is likely to involve working for a living. STEM skills are highly valued by employers, who frequently report difficulties in recruiting suitably qualified staff. Across Europe, it is estimated that there will be 7 million jobs that require STEM skills by 2025 (an increase of 8% compared to 3% across all employment types). The more teachers can do to promote a positive image of STEM and nurture positive attitudes, the more chance there will be an adequate supply of adults with STEM skills in the future. You can find a wealth of information about STEM careers on the internet (e.g. www.futuremorph.org) that can be easily incorporated into the learning experiences you offer.

Despite the role of STEM in modern society, it is a concern among most Western governments that many students do not choose to study STEM subjects post-16 or at university. Recent UK government initiatives concerned with STEM have focused on 14- and 15-year-olds, but the research evidence suggests this is too late. Children's attitudes towards mathematics and science form relatively early (Tytler et al., 2008) and decline as they get older (Sturman et al., 2012). The ASPIRES project (www.kcl.ac.uk/aspires) has investigated children's career aspirations and found that children's attitudes towards STEM careers are often fixed by age ten. Home has a particularly important role to play in shaping children's attitudes to STEM and whether they are likely to develop and sustain STEM related aspirations.

STEM SKILLS

STEM skills are essential for STEM literacy. They are transferable skills valuable to all learners and highly prized by employers. There is no single agreed definition of STEM skills but the list below draws on definitions from across Europe.

1. Be creative and imaginative

2. Ask questions, pose problems, hypothesise, conjecture

3. Devise and conduct experiments to investigate situations and test hypotheses

4. Devise strategies to solve problems and carry them out making adjustments as necessary

5. Seek patterns and relationships and explain them

6. Work cooperatively with others

7. Apply appropriate mathematical techniques to collect and analyse data

8. Construct arguments using scientific and mathematical knowledge

9. Research information and check its veracity

10. Communicate effectively for different purposes in a range of contexts

11. Use tools, equipment, software and materials safely

12. Evaluate their work and identify ways it might be improved

A hypothesis is a statement based on limited evidence that can be tested by experiment or data collection, for example 'a polystyrene cup keeps a drink colder for longer' or 'girls eat more healthily than boys'.

A conjecture is a statement based on evidence that has not been proved, for example, 'even square numbers are multiples of four'.

TEACHING STEM

Primary schools are in an ideal position to nurture positive attitudes towards STEM through using rich starting points to develop rigorous learning in mathematics, science and technology. From conducting experiments on the best container for a hot drink, to designing and making a timer for boiling an egg, the primary curriculum can incorporate principles of design, experimentation and data analysis through practical, meaningful activities. Children can explore imaginative or fanciful questions such as:

- How big is a dinosaur?

- Would a whale fit in the school hall?

- How long would it take to count to a million?

- Why can we only see one side of the Moon?

- How can I make a sundial?

- How much water do I use every day compared with someone in Africa?

Primary schools generally have good home-school links and are particularly well placed to foster and build positive dispositions towards STEM within and beyond the curriculum. Nurturing positive attitudes and dispositions towards STEM in the primary school is essential to prepare young people for living in our modern, global and increasingly technological society. As resilient and optimistic STEM learners in primary school, they are more likely to sustain their interest through adolescence.

Many primary schools are embracing curriculum approaches that focus on whole child development such as Guy Claxton's building learning power (Claxton, 2002; focusing on resilience, resourcefulness, reflectiveness and reciprocity), Neil Hawkes's values-based education (www.neilhawkes.org) and Matthew Lipman's philosophy for children (Lipman, 1976). These approaches have the potential to contribute to nurturing positive learner identities across the curriculum, particularly in science and mathematics. By encouraging learners to ask their own questions, explore alternatives and appreciate diverse perspectives and outcomes, children can experience mathematics and science as exciting and creative subjects. These approaches exemplify Vygotsky's and Bruner's ideas around social constructivism, suggesting that learning is a personal activity that happens with others. Dweck's *Growth Mindset* (2008) is also important as children who believe in their capacity to learn are far more likely to do so. Teacher expectations are important too. Holistic approaches suggest we should believe in our children and give them the opportunity to surprise us with what they can actually do.

The teacher's role as the main source of knowledge and information is changing. In the age of the internet and sophisticated search engines, information is readily available. It has never been essential that, as a teacher, you know the answers to all the questions that children pose, and today it is even less so. Teachers need to be nurturing children's confidence and critical literacy skills to enable them to interrogate information and ask:

- How true?

- What do others say?

- Could I ask my question in a different way?

Using questions to challenge children's thinking and provoke explanations is increasingly important. Designing activities that require children to work collaboratively and discuss with one another will help to secure learning, raise achievement and develop positive attitudes (Boaler, n.d.). All of this requires a secure and supportive learning environment where the teacher has high expectations for all and in which children can take intellectual risks without fear of ridicule from other children or the teacher.

Activities that provide motivating and challenging opportunities for learning based on mathematics, science, technology and engineering can enrich the curriculum and help to increase coherence for learners. Drawing on expertise outside the school through STEM ambassadors (www.stemnet.org.uk/content/stem-ambassadors) and the STEM directories (www.stemdirectories.org.uk) can strengthen community links and raise children's aspirations. There are useful websites on careers in STEM (stemcareer.com) and mathematics (www.mathscareers.org.uk). NRICH hosts a range of STEM resources.

STEM IN PRACTICE

Below are some examples of what STEM teaching looks like in the primary context:

- If you want children to make a model of a cuboid, rather than providing a net to cut out and glue, you might offer a range of cuboid packaging and ask them to decide how to make their own net. They could do this by working collaboratively and experimenting with different designs. The outcome might include a display of all the different nets that work.

- If you want to establish a school vegetable garden, you might invite the local allotment society (or similar) to come and work with the children to do this.

- If you want to teach the relative sizes of planets and distance from the sun you might challenge the children to investigate and create a scale model. They may decide they want to visit a planetarium and they could organise the visit themselves.

- If you want children to do a piece of original scientific research you might look for a current 'citizen science' project (e.g. www.opalexplorenature.org/surveys) and get a real scientist involved. Look at rsbl.royalsocietypublishing.org/content/7/2/168 to find an example of children doing original research and even getting published in a Royal Society journal!

- If you want children to design and market a healthy snack, you might get a local business to work with the children on the market research and a food scientist to help evaluate it.

These are not new ideas. In 1982 the Cockroft report (*Mathematics Counts*) stated:

There is general agreement that understanding in mathematics implies an ability to recognise and to make use of a mathematical concept in a variety of settings, including some which are not immediately familiar ...

(p. 68)

... Because understanding is an internal state of mind which has to be achieved individually by each pupil, it cannot be observed directly by the teacher. The fact that a pupil is able to solve a particular problem correctly does not necessarily indicate that understanding of the relevant concepts is present. A much better indication of the depth of understanding which exists can be obtained in the course of discussion, by means of appropriate practical work or through more general problem-solving activities ...

(p. 69)

... Research shows that these three elements – facts and skills, conceptual structures, general strategies and appreciation – involve distinct aspects of teaching and require separate attention. It follows that effective mathematics teaching must pay attention to all three ...

(p. 71)

... Mathematics teaching at all levels should include opportunities for

- exposition by the teacher;
- discussion between teacher and learners and between learners themselves;
- appropriate practical work;
- consolidation and practice of fundamental skills and routines;
- problem solving, including the application of mathematics to everyday situations;
- investigational work.

(p. 71)

and in 1998, Nuffield's *Beyond 2000: Science Education for the Future* stated:

... pupils should come to see science as a search for reliable explanations of the behaviour of the natural world. Their understanding of science should come from:

- evaluating, interpreting and analysing both evidence which has been collected first-hand and evidence which has been obtained from secondary sources;
- hearing and reading stories about how important ideas were first developed and became established and accepted;
- learning how to construct sound and persuasive arguments based upon evidence;
- considering a range of current issues involving the application of science and scientific ideas.

(p. 21)

... it is important to emphasise our view that the science curriculum of the future should have much greater variety, not only in the types of learning activity involved but also in the pace of learning. Any science curriculum which is essentially a list of concepts is bound to be content-focused. If the accompanying modes of assessment have a similar narrow focus, then the combination will force some teachers into a rigid transmissive mode of teaching. One unfortunate consequence is a denial of opportunities for pupils to conduct extended pieces of work exploring aspects of the history of science, or to examine media reports of socio-scientific controversies which report aspects of contemporary science, risk and controversy.

(p. 23)

THREE KEY DEBATES

Despite these long-standing exhortations for science and mathematics education to include problem solving, practical work and exploration, the controversy around how best to teach science and mathematics continues. Three key debates are summarised below.

1 'SCIENCE/MATHEMATICS FOR CITIZENS' VERSUS 'SCIENCE/MATHEMATICS FOR SCIENTISTS/MATHEMATICIANS'

Some argue that future (research) scientists and mathematicians have different needs from those of citizens who use science and mathematics 'only' for making informed decisions in our increasingly technological and science based society.

Learning *about* science and mathematics is important to all future citizens. It provides a framework within which to understand and organise their science and mathematics skills, understanding and knowledge. This enables them to learn more effectively and apply what they learn, now and in the future. Professional scientists and mathematicians are increasingly specialists operating in multi-disciplinary teams and to be effective it is essential that they have a secure grounding in the breadth of science and mathematics as well as in-depth knowledge of their specialist areas. So, scientists and mathematicians need what citizens need together with preparation to practise their specialism. The latter on its own 'sells them short' both as future researchers and as citizens. In the past, science and mathematics for citizens have focused largely on how the two subjects work as domains of knowledge and on their applications. It may be that for the future they also need to include more about the place of science and mathematics in our wider culture and their role in the economic wellbeing of our nation.

2 LEARNING INDIVIDUAL COMPONENTS OF EACH NEW TOPIC SEPARATELY VERSUS LEARNING DIFFERENT COMPONENTS TOGETHER

It is quite a common belief that learners always need new topics broken down into 'manageable' pieces that they can put together and use once they have practised them sufficiently. Others believe that learning can be approached more holistically through tackling engaging problems and developing new understandings or skills, or acquiring information, as required.

Theories of learning and new discoveries about how the brain works offer little support for the view that new components must be learned separately and thoroughly before they can be combined into useful outcomes. Children say they learn better if they can see how what they are currently learning relates to what they are learning elsewhere and to what they already know. Learning components separately does not provide opportunities for children to experience and understand the different ways that scientific theories and mathematics have been developed, e.g. the use of inductive and deductive reasoning and the use of models, concepts and analogies.

3 TRADITIONAL LEARNING OF SCIENCE AND MATHEMATICS VERSUS PREPARATION FOR A RAPIDLY CHANGING FUTURE GLOBAL SOCIETY

Some argue that to produce great scientists/mathematicians such as those in our past and those we have today we need to give learners the same kind of learning experience they had. Others believe that an education based on factual science, technical competence at mathematics procedures and limited practical skills will not equip learners to practise science or mathematics effectively in a future world.

In today's world, information is available at the touch of a button and scientific knowledge in an area of science can double on a timescale of months rather than decades and go out of date overnight. Future scientists do need scientific knowledge, partly as a basis to judge the value of new information they acquire. However, this does not need to be as extensive as in the past, with skills and understanding having equal or greater importance. Scientists particularly need the skills to effectively communicate their ideas to scientists from other backgrounds, to co-workers who are not scientists and to the public.

CONCLUSION

STEM education is inclusive and emancipatory. In focusing on issues and challenges, it allows learners to appreciate the power of STEM to solve problems with understanding and responsibility. It exposes links and connections that help learners to appreciate how decisions have ramifications that need to be considered before action is taken. Watching a video about the impact of damming the Yangtze River in China and comparing that with the creation of Tilberthwaite Reservoir in the Lake District in the 1930s allows students to appreciate how STEM crosses boundaries of culture and time.

In this book, we have drawn together exciting starting points for STEM education in the primary school. Primary schools are well placed to plan curriculum opportunities that blur subject boundaries, ensuring coherent rich experiences for children that can be exploited for learning across the curriculum and in specific subjects. Typically, these experiences will involve children working in teams or groups that may be mixed age. They may involve going off site or working with visitors to the school. They need the same thorough planning that you usually do, taking account of individual needs and completing risk assessments as necessary. The benefits of such experiences can permeate the curriculum, being re-visited in many different lessons to support learning. For example, a paper plane competition will generate data that can be used in computing and mathematics lessons, plane designs that can be evaluated in science and D&T. It will build personal skills of co-operation, persistence, resilience and practical skills of making and measuring.

Every activity describes the preparation you need to undertake, the potential links to different subjects and how you might adapt and develop it for your learners. We hope that you enjoy this book and that it inspires you to develop STEM literate learners.

THE BOOK CHAPTERS

Chapter 1 by Amanda Smith introduces activities that can be completed by children at home and discussed in class, as a means of building school-home links that will help to foster positive dispositions towards STEM.

Chapter 2 by Eleanor Hoskins shows how practical activities in the early years can build foundations for later STEM learning.

In Chapter 3, Rania Maklad shares stimulating starting points for scientific exploration.

Mathematics is the focus for STEM learning in Chapter 4 by Sue Pope.

Chapter 5 by Ben Sedman and Anne Guilford uses design and technology as the starting point for practical activities that develop a range of skills.

In Chapter 6, Pauline Palmer and Sarah Lister illustrate how the CLIL approach for language and content acquisition can be used to enhance STEM learning.

Chapter 7 by Rebecca Patterson, Mick Chesterman and Alison Ramsay uses drama to explore STEM literacy development.

In Chapter 8, Helen Caldwell, Sway Grantham and Neil Smith explore how engaging girls in STEM can help to build confident resilient learners through inclusive classroom practices.

Yasemin Allsop discusses the silent C in STEM and shows how computing can enhance STEM learning in Chapter 9.

Chapter 10 by Helen Caldwell, Jean Edwards and Sway Grantham focuses on enhancing STEM education using the arts (STEAM).

David Barlex concludes the book in Chapter 11 with activities designed to support transition to secondary school.

REFERENCES

Boaler, J. (n.d.) *Jo Boaler Explains Complex Instruction*. Available at https://nrich.maths.org/7013.

Claxton, G. (2002) *Building Learning Power*. Bristol: TLO.

Cockroft, W. H. (1982) *Mathematics Counts*. London: HMSO.

Dweck, C. (2008) *Mindset*. New York: Ballantine Books.

Lipman, M. (1976) Philosophy for Children. *Metaphilosophy*, 7(1), 17-33.

Nuffield Foundation (1998) *Beyond 2000: Science Education for the Future*. London: Nuffield Foundation.

Royal Society (2014) *Vision for Science and Mathematics Education*. London: Royal Society.

Sturman, L., Burge, B., Cook, R. & Weaving, H. (2012) *TIMSS 2011: Mathematics and Science Achievement in England*. Slough: NFER.

Tytler, R. et al. (2008) *Opening Up Pathways: Engagement in STEM across the Primary-Secondary School Transition*. Available at https://docs.education.gov.au/system/files/doc/other/openpathinscitechmathengin primsecschtrans.pdf (accessed April 2016).

FURTHER READING

Banks, F. & Barlex, D. (2014) *Teaching STEM in the Secondary School*. Abingdon: Routledge.

Cross, A. & Borthwick, A. (2016) *Connecting Primary Maths & Science*. London: Open University Press.

WEBSITES

STEM Central Scotland: www.educationscotland.gov.uk/stemcentral/about/curriculum/index.asp

STEM careers starting point: https://nationalcareersservice.direct.gov.uk/aboutus/newsarticles/Pages/ stem/STEM-careers-booming-opportunities-making-a-difference.aspx

1
STEM AND MAKING LINKS WITH HOME

AMANDA SMITH

INTRODUCTION

There is considerable evidence that when families see STEM subjects as 'hard' or 'boring' rather than 'exciting' and 'full of potential', children are less likely to engage with and see STEM as being for them (Smith, 2002; NIACE, 2013; Macdonald, 2014). Support from families and carers is vital if more children are to opt for STEM subjects.

This need to engage families and carers in the STEM-related learning of children is addressed in science via a number of projects and resources. Examples include *Learning Science Together, Science Opens Doors*, the Institute of Physics' *Marvin and Milo* cards, *Science Sparks* and *Pop up Physics for Families*. All focus on encouraging curiosity and hands on exploration.

IN THIS CHAPTER

In this chapter, I focus on the *SCRUFF* project. This project not only engages families in science learning, it explicitly attempts to set up a positive dialogue within the family about science learning, a dialogue that is structured and reinforced by the school through the use of the SCRUFF resources. This is an approach to strengthen home–school learning that can be used across all STEM disciplines.

The activities presented in the second half of this chapter are inspired by the work of the SCRUFF project. They are intended to stimulate scientific thinking and discussion through practical activities completed at home, and will help you to enhance the attitudes and confidence of the children in your class.

There are a range of activities for children in the primary years that encourage scientific thinking and exploration.

SCRUFF

Science for Children Ready to Use with Family and Friends (SCRUFF) comprises a set of science based teaching and learning materials designed to be used by children at home, with introduction and follow-up in school. SCRUFF has been created collaboratively by the Centre for STEM Education at Manchester Metropolitan University and its partner Primarily Science. The SCRUFF approach involves mapping the attitudes of children and their families towards science learning and tracking how they change as families engage in fun, interactive science activities together. The school plays a central role in structuring, driving and consolidating this learning process. The process has resulted in significant improvement in family attitudes towards children's STEM learning with more active support and encouragement being offered with homework and ultimately with subject choice (Smith, 2002).

SCRUFF IN PRACTICE

SCRUFF has a 'comic book' appearance led by an appealing cartoon dog character who likes to go on adventures and make discoveries. The project is introduced in school and children take home activities to work on with a family member or carer. Where this is not possible, children are encouraged to work with a friend or an older child from the school. The activities are easy to run and the resources needed readily found in most homes. The purpose of each activity is not to arrive at a 'correct answer' but to have fun by investigating, observing and exploring together. The teacher's effective direction of the project is vital to its success.

The project takes place over a six-week period. The teacher initiates it by an explanatory letter home introducing the project, with a 'find out' meeting for children and families. The opening activity is a questionnaire for children to use with their families to explore their own experience and attitudes towards science. This is followed by fun weekly investigations with the teacher preparing the children to lead the activity in the home. The teacher follows up on the activity to consolidate learning, pursue ideas and questions and to talk about what it was like working on science at home. Children and their learning partner (family member or carer) are encouraged to keep a SCRUFF diary; this can provide good evidence of engagement and learning for all those involved. The final activity is a questionnaire where children and their partners reflect on what it has been like to work together and how their engagement and attitudes have changed.

SCRUFF AND MEASURING ENGAGEMENT

In relation to the pre- and post-questionnaires on engagement and attitudes to science, the teacher is key in ensuring the children are well prepared to lead on these activities with their learning partner at home. In effect, the teacher conducts and models an interview with the children about their own engagement and attitudes to science learning. The interview comprises a series of straightforward questions that tease out the science they have done in school and how they approached it, and confirms that these approaches are scientific. This will help children to identify the scientific content they have explored and the scientific methods they have used, such as observing, experimenting, making predictions, investigating and so on. Finally, children should be encouraged to make statements about their attitudes to their science learning so far using open ended questions such as:

- 'What do you think of science?'

- 'Did you enjoy it and if so why?'

- 'Do you think science is important?'

- 'Have you learned any science outside of school?'

Children often draw on their experience of science in the media here. For example, there are a range of children's television programmes as well as magazines and books related to science. The interview may be supported by a writing frame using number scales and word fields that children draw on to help them structure their responses. The resultant information can be treated as a collection of data for the school to evaluate the affective impact of their science provision on the children. The key messages are then fed back to the group to help build a dialogue about their science learning to date.

A similar questionnaire can be developed with the children for use with their family learning partner. The teacher will have access to this for analysis. The teacher casts the children as interviewers and encourages them to use a recording device such as a smart phone to capture the interview. The interview itself focuses on experiences that we all have in common through questions such as:

- 'Did you learn science at school?'

- 'What did you think of it?'

- 'How did you learn it?'

- 'What sorts of things did you do?'

- 'Did you like science?'

- 'Have you learned any science since you left school?'

- 'Do you think science is important?'

Children report back on what they found out in the interview during the follow-up in school. They can use the recording to remind themselves of the key points and help focus their report. The teacher's role is to draw out the key differences and similarities between the responses the children gave about science and those of their family members.

When all the SCRUFF activities have been completed at home (usually one a week for six weeks), the final interviews are conducted. In school, the teacher draws out the learning from the project and what difference it has made to the children to work on science with someone at home. The children then interview their learning partner and try to draw out the benefits of the science experience they have shared using questions such as:

- 'What did you find interesting?'

- 'Did you enjoy the investigations?'

- 'Was it different to the way you learned science at school?'

- 'Did you enjoy us working together?'

The learning pair should look at the recording grid and interview they made at the start and see if anything has changed. In a similar way, the teacher debriefs on the key findings and these are used to construct a concluding letter that celebrates the impact of the project with participating families. Some schools have a celebration event to talk about the experiences they have had. The intention here is to consolidate an on-going relationship between the child and their learning partner around their STEM experiences in school.

The activities in this chapter are designed to be completed by children working with their learning partner at home. The teacher needs to spend time introducing each activity and then discussing children's experiences.

ACTIVITY

Get the Point?

What you need to know

At home, children and their learning partners work scientifically to investigate the differences in sensitivity of some areas of the skin to touch. They draw conclusions from their experimental findings and consider why different parts of the skin show differing sensitivities to touch. The final activity requires the learning team to consider the findings of recent scientific research and carry out an investigation to explore why fingertips go wrinkly in water.

Preparation

Objectives: Exploring which part of the hand and arm are most sensitive to touch

Curriculum links: Working scientifically – investigating everyday phenomena, conducting a fair test, recording and discussing outcomes

Year groups: Suitable for years 3 to 4. Older children might extend the skin sensitivity investigation to other parts of the body – they could form and test a hypothesis

Equipment: Paperclip and ruler. Marbles and warm water for the follow-up activity

Useful links

STEM Education centre website: www2.mmu.ac.uk/stem

Primarily science website: www.primarilyscience.co.uk

ASE website: www.ase.org.uk

Setting the scene

When dogs are born they cannot see or hear. The first sense SCRUFF developed was the sense of touch. SCRUFF has very sensitive pads on her feet and whiskers above her eyes that are sensitive to air flow. She also loves to be stroked!

Humans also learn a great deal about the world around them from their sense of touch. Our skin contains lots of tiny touch sensors but some areas of the skin have more touch sensors than others. This experiment will be done at home with a family member or friend. We will call them your partner. You will investigate which parts of your body are the most sensitive to touch.

Trigger questions

- Can you design an investigation to find out which part of your hand or arm is most sensitive to touch?

- Which part of your hand and arm do you think might be the most sensitive to touch?

- Why?

Time to experiment at home

Sit down with your partner in a quiet place.

Bend a paperclip or hair pin into a horseshoe shape until the points are 5 mm apart.

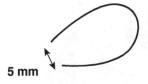

5 mm

(Continued)

(Continued)

How sensitive is your forearm?

Forearm

Ask your partner to close their eyes and keep them closed.

Gently touch your partner's forearm with either one or two points of the paperclip. Your partner has to guess how many points they feel each time.

Touch them 5 times with one or two points (you decide) and count how many times they get it right. Make a note of the score out of 5.

Now swap places and repeat the experiment. You close your eyes and your partner will test you with one or two points of the clip.

Make a note of your scores out of 5.

How many did each of you get right out of 5 goes?

How sensitive is the back of your hand?

Ask your partner to close their eyes and keep them closed.

This time touch the back of your partner's hand 5 times with one or two points.

Count how many times they get it right.

Back of hand

Now swap places and repeat the experiment. You close your eyes and your partner will test you with one or two points of the clip.

Make a note of your scores. How many did each of you get right out of 5 goes?

How sensitive is your fingertip?

Ask your partner to close their eyes and keep them closed.

This time touch your partner's fingertip 5 times with one or two points.

Count how many times they get it right.

Fingertip

Now swap places and repeat the experiment. You close your eyes and your partner will test you with one or two points of the clip.

Make a note of your scores. How many did each of you get right out of 5 goes?

Review and reflect

Look at the scores.

Did you notice any patterns? What did you observe in your scores?

Of the three areas you tested:

- Which was the most sensitive part of the skin for you?
- Which was the most sensitive part of the skin for your partner?
- Which was the least sensitive part of the skin for you?
- Which was the least sensitive part of the skin for your partner?
- Which part of your skin do you think contains the most touch sensors?
- Why do you think this part of the skin contains the most touch sensors?

(Continued)

(Continued)

Assessment

The teacher can use the responses to the activity questions in order to assess the outcomes.

They can carry out a debriefing session where children can share their findings, observations and ideas.

A SCRUFF diary might be completed by the child and family member to reflect on the experiment, and evaluate their findings and enjoyment of the activity.

The same can be done for the follow-up activity.

Follow-up activities

Why do fingertips go wrinkly in the bath?

Have you ever noticed that your fingertips go wrinkly when you spend a long time in the bath?

Discuss with your partner what they look and feel like.

Do your arms and legs go wrinkly too?

What about your toes and feet?

Why do you think this wrinkling happens?

Jot down some of your ideas. Do not worry about getting a right or wrong answer. Try and think of as many ideas as you can, even if they seem wild!

Here is some interesting information:

Scientists have found that if the touch sensors are damaged on a fingertip it does not wrinkle in water!

ACTIVITY

How good are wrinkly fingers at picking up objects?

Experiment 1

Time how long it takes you to pick up and move 20 dry marbles one at a time from one bowl to another.

Time how long it takes you to pick up and move 20 wet marbles one at a time from one bowl to another.

Which was the fastest? Did you find it easier to pick up the dry or wet marbles?

Now let your partner have a go.

How did you make sure this was a fair test?

Experiment 2

Now soak your hands in warm water for about 20 minutes or have a bath!

Repeat the experiment above with your wrinkly fingers.

Which was the fastest? Did you find it easier to pick up the dry or wet marbles?

Now let your partner have a go.

What did you and your partner find interesting in your results?

Did you notice any patterns?

Why do you think this happened?

What ideas have you now got about why fingers go wrinkly in water?

ACTIVITY

SCRUFF's floaters and sinkers

What you need to know

At home, children and their learning partners work scientifically to explore floating and sinking with everyday objects. They look for patterns in the properties of the floaters and the sinkers. The activity is extended to consider what happens to fruit in water when its peel is removed. The follow-up activity aims to surprise the learning team and provoke ideas and conversation that leads to an exploration related to density. This activity does not include a scientific explanation of density.

Preparation

Objectives: Exploring floating and sinking

Curriculum links: Working scientifically – investigating everyday phenomena, conducting a fair test, recording and discussing outcomes

Year groups: Year 1 upwards. Older learners could use Plasticine to investigate whether different shapes float or sink, e.g. a hollowed out bowl or a compact solid shape

Equipment: Sink, bowl or tank, small objects made from different materials, e.g. spoon, pen, coin, paper, cotton wool, wood, plastic, orange and any fruit that will peel, lemonade or any clear fizzy drink, 6 raisins or sultanas

Useful links

STEM Education centre website: www2.mmu.ac.uk/stem

Primarily science website: www.primarilyscience.co.uk

ASE website: www.ase.org.uk

Setting the scene

SCRUFF likes to swim and fetch her ball in water. She has a special ball that is light and full of air. Some objects stay on top of water; this is called floating. SCRUFF's ball floats on water so she can see it easily.

We say objects sink when they fall to the bottom in water. It is not always easy to guess which objects will float or sink in water so we need to test them. You are going to investigate floating and sinking with a family member or friend. We will call them your partner.

Trigger questions

- Think about objects that you have seen floating. What do you think objects that float have in common?

- Now think about objects that you have seen sinking. What do you think sinking objects have in common?

- Can you design an investigation to find out which objects float and which sink?

Time to experiment at home

Everyday floaters and sinkers

Collect some small objects made from different materials.

Fill a bowl, sink, tank or bath with water.

With your partner decide which objects you think will float and which will sink.

Sort them into two piles.

Drop the objects into the water one at a time.

Watch what happens.

Which objects float? Is there anything similar about them?

Which objects sink? Have you spotted anything similar about these objects?

Can you find a way to make floaters sink and sinkers float?

(Continued)

(Continued)

Fruity floaters and sinkers

Now try putting an orange into the water. Does it float or sink?

Why do you think this happens?

Peel the orange and put it back in the water. Does it float or sink?

Why do you think this happens?

Place the peel in the water. Does it float or sink?

Why do you think this happens?

Try the same experiment with different fruits that you can peel, e.g. apples, bananas and lemons.

What do you observe? Can you explain why?

Review and reflect

- Discuss your findings with your partner.
- What have you noticed about things that float?
- Do all the things that sink have something in common?
- How would you explain floating and sinking to someone else?

Assessment

The teacher can use the responses to the activity questions to assess the outcomes.

They can carry out a debriefing session where children can share their findings, observations and ideas.

A SCRUFF diary might be completed by the child and family member to reflect on the experiment, and evaluate their findings and enjoyment of the activity.

The same can be done for the follow-up activity.

Follow-up activity

Sinking sultanas

Pour some lemonade or clear fizzy drink into a glass.

What do you think will happen if you drop six sultanas (or raisins) into the lemonade? Will they float or sink?

Drop the sultanas into the lemonade and observe very carefully what happens.

Look closely at the sultanas. What can you see forming on their surface?

Discuss with your partner what you have observed. Can you explain what is happening?

ACTIVITY

Blowing for gold!

What you need to know

At home, children and their learning partners work scientifically to investigate the relationship between height and lung capacity (i.e. how much air your lungs can hold).

The learning team investigate lung capacity by measuring how far a tin foil ball can be blown across a surface using a drinking straw, following a deep intake of breath. They are encouraged to involve other family members and friends to collect a range of results and look for patterns.

(Continued)

(Continued)

Finding ways to measure how much air you can breathe in or blow out can help us find out how much air your lungs can hold.

Preparation

Objective: Investigation to find out whether your height affects how much air your lungs can hold

Curriculum links: Working scientifically, conducting a fair test, measuring and recording data, drawing conclusions from data

Year groups: Years 3 and 4. Older learners could record their results in a spreadsheet and investigate representing their data in a graph

Equipment: 2 drinking straws, tape measure or ruler, small piece of kitchen foil rolled into a ball

Useful links

STEM Education centre website: www2.mmu.ac.uk/stem

Primarily science website: www.primarilyscience.co.uk

ASE website: www.ase.org.uk

Setting the scene

When SCRUFF gets very excited she pants. The air goes in and out of her small lungs as she breathes in and out.

Do you think bigger dogs have bigger lungs that can hold more air?

You have two lungs and they are so big they take up most of the room in your chest. They are protected by a set of bones called your rib cage. Place your hands on your chest and breathe in and out slowly and deeply. Feel your chest move upwards as your lungs fill with air. Doctors can tell how well our lungs are working by asking us to take in a deep breath and then blowing out air as fast and long as you can. The amount of air you can blow out tells us about how much air your lungs can hold.

Trigger questions

- Do you think big lungs can take in and breathe out more air than small lungs?
- Do you think taller people have bigger lungs than shorter people?
- If a person breathes in deeply, how can we test how much air they can blow out in one go? What kinds of things could we observe or measure?

Time to experiment at home

Let's investigate how much air you can blow in one breath.

Take a drinking straw each and make a small ball with some kitchen foil.

Practise blowing the foil ball along a flat surface, like a table top or the floor.

Blow the ball back and forth to each other.

Next, hold your straw and place the foil ball in front of you on the flat surface.

Take a deep breath in and with one big blow through the straw, see how far you can blow the ball across the surface. Use a ruler or tape measure to find out how far the ball travelled in cm. Do this one at a time, using the same ball and surface. Place the ball in the same place in front of you each time.

Use a tape measure or ruler to measure your heights in cm.

Can you find more family members or friends to take part in your investigation? Have a competition to see who can blow the ball the furthest.

You could record your results on a table like this one:

Name	Height in cm	Distance travelled in cm

Review and reflect

- Why should you keep the ball, surface and starting point the same?
- Who was the tallest?
- Who was the shortest?

(Continued)

(Continued)

- Who could blow the ball the furthest?
- Did you notice any patterns in your results?
- Who do you think has the biggest lung capacity (whose lungs can hold the most air)?
- Do you think taller people have a bigger lung capacity than shorter people?

Assessment

The teacher can use the responses to the activity questions to assess the outcomes.

They can carry out a debriefing session where children can share their findings, observations and ideas.

A SCRUFF diary might be completed by the child and family member to reflect on the experiment, and evaluate their findings and enjoyment of the activity.

The same can be done for the follow-up activity.

Follow-up activities

What other factors might affect how far the ball will travel?

Design your own investigation. Here are some ideas of things you might explore:

- Surface the ball travels on.
- Size of the ball.
- Size of the straw.

Can you design and make a good game to play using the kit from this investigation?

If someone playing your game is taller, have they got a better chance of winning the game?

Involving family members in practical activities at home can stimulate conversations that help to build children's confidence and attitude towards science. Completing the SCRUFF diary together provides a basis for dialogue with the home that puts children's learning foremost.

Children's attitudes towards STEM form early, and parents or carers have a profound influence (Archer Ker et al., 2013: ASPIRES project). Providing enjoyable shared experiences can make a real difference.

REFERENCES

Archer Ker, L., DeWitt, J., Osborne, J. F., Dillon, J. S., Wong, B. & Willis, B. (2013) *ASPIRES Report: Young People's Science and Career Aspirations, Age 10-14*. London: King's College London.

Macdonald, A. (2014) *'Not for People Like Me?' Under-represented Groups in Science, Technology and Engineering: A Summary of the Evidence: The Facts, the Fiction and What We Should Do Next*. Leeds: WISE.

NIACE (2013) *Family Learning Works*. Leicester: National Institute of Adult Continuing Education.

Smith, A. (2002) *Evaluating the Impact of a Science Homework Project Where Parents and Children Work Together as Partners*. Best Practice Research Scholarship. London: DfES.

FURTHER READING

Association for Science Education (2016) Family learning. *Primary Science*, 143.

Lydon, S. & King, C. (2009) Can a single professional development workshop cause change in the classroom? *Professional Development in Education*, 35(1), 65-82.

WEBSITES

Learning Science Together: https://pstt.org.uk/resources/curriculum-materials/learning-science-together

Institute of Physics, 'Marvin and Milo': www.physics.org/marvinandmilo.asp

Science Sparks: www.science-sparks.com

2

STEM IN THE EARLY YEARS

ELEANOR HOSKINS

The foundations of formal learning begin in the early years, and this is where we can sow the seeds of systematic exploration and investigation. In the early years, children need opportunities to follow their own independent paths of curiosity and develop an understanding of investigation through trialling ideas. Continuous provision, where learning is 'continued' in the absence of an adult, provides many opportunities for key independent learning through trial and improve. Such trial-and-improve explorations and investigations, when linked to the world around us, can ignite an ongoing interest in STEM and lay firm foundations for future formal teaching and learning.

IN THIS CHAPTER

In this chapter, STEM subjects within early years education are explored through continuous provision projects. Child-led activities are designed to develop young children's knowledge, skills and understanding within the early explorations of science, technology, engineering and mathematics. The activities are intended to inspire young children to engage with STEM areas linked to the world around them and to lay firm foundations for subject knowledge development in future learning.

THE EYFS

The Statutory Framework for the Early Years Foundation Stage (EYFS) of 2017 outlines seven areas of learning and development, under the headings of 'Prime' and 'Specific' areas.

PRIME AREAS

- Communication and language (listening and attention, understanding, speaking).
- Physical development (moving and handling, health and self-care).

- Personal, social and emotional development (self-confidence and self-awareness, managing feelings and behaviour, making relationships).

SPECIFIC AREAS

- Literacy (reading, writing).

- Mathematics (numbers, shapes, spaces and measures).

- Understanding the world (people and communities, the world, technology).

- Expressive arts and design (exploring and using media and materials, being imaginative).

The STEM subjects mainly fit within the 'specific' areas of 'Mathematics' and 'Understanding the world' with some links to 'Expressive arts and design'. However, this does not mean STEM subjects should be explored through these specific areas alone, since all seven areas should interrelate where possible.

The specific areas from the framework (as listed above) are a vehicle through which the prime areas are strengthened and applied, so every STEM activity should also link to one or more prime areas where possible. This enables the children to continue developing prime area key skills and capabilities while developing their STEM subject knowledge simultaneously.

For each continuous provision project outlined in this chapter, clear EYFS links are provided. All projects in this chapter are designed to be incorporated within the setting as part of continuous provision. The core aim for each activity is to develop children's independent exploration and investigation skills, but it is often helpful to model how the resources can be used during a group activity before introducing the activity into the setting.

For each continuous provision project, there are ideas outlined for assessment. With young children, the preferred assessment approach is to gather 'in the moment' evidence. This often includes photographs, videos, short observations or small scribbled notes as the children engage with the activities. This approach permits evidence gathering that can then be added to electronic or paper learning journeys and measured against age appropriate goals, without interrupting any essential exploratory learning.

BUILDINGS AND CONSTRUCTION

The STEM continuous provision projects outlined in this chapter all relate to the theme of Buildings and Construction. This topic provides many opportunities for young children to explore STEM-related subjects associated with the world around them though exploratory play. The importance of exploratory play lies in the opportunities provided to establish firm foundations for future knowledge and understanding. The beginnings of core concepts associated with the STEM subjects such as structural building, properties of materials, computer programming and mathematical reasoning can begin through basic trial and improve in an exploratory play context. Free-thinking trial-and-improve play ignites interest in young children's minds, stores information and, as a result, provides firm foundations for later formal teaching and learning.

ACTIVITY

Beautiful buildings

What you need to know

The 'beautiful building' activity is designed as outside (Coloursplash Buildings) and inside (Sensory Construction Site) continuous provision. The outside activity relies on some sun, so consider the time of year. For the outside activity, it would be helpful if children had some experience of making shadows. This prior experience will help stimulate their interest to explore shadow making further.

Preparation

Objectives

- To recognise characteristics of everyday shapes and use these for construction.
- To explore similarities and differences between materials.

EYFS links

Physical development

Moving and handling - good control and coordination of colour blocks.

Personal, social and emotional development

Self-confidence and self-awareness - building confidence to try new activities. Making relationships - playing cooperatively, taking turns, forming positive relationships with others while playing and exploring.

Understanding the world

Similarities and differences related to objects and materials.

Mathematics

Shapes, spaces and measures - characteristics of everyday shapes.

Suitable for: Children aged 3 and above.

Equipment

Coloursplash Buildings - wooden, sensory building blocks contain coloured Perspex windows and variations in texture with glitter and liquid. If you do not have a set of these sensory blocks then make your own using cardboard and coloured cellophane.

Sensory Construction Site - add extra resources to the sand tray, such as gravel, rocks, pebbles, glass beads, washers alongside toy diggers and trucks.

Useful links

To purchase wooden sensory blocks: www.sensoryplus.co.uk/products/wooden-toys/sensory-blocks-set-of-16/SE826

Setting the scene

Coloursplash Buildings - If the children have visited shadow making before, opportunities to reignite their interest about making shadows during group interaction would work well before this activity.

Sensory Construction Site - In small groups, discuss with the children what a construction site looks like and the materials often seen.

Trigger questions

- Look carefully at the shapes of the blocks. Which are the same and which are different?
- Look carefully at the shadows of the blocks on the ground. Do they look the same or different to the blocks?
- Why would a construction site have lots of sand, gravel, rocks and stones?

Time to experiment

Coloursplash Buildings

Set up the sensory building blocks outside in a big space to allow children to explore without space restrictions. It is often a good idea to produce some photographs to prompt the children with their independent explorations while still allowing them to investigate freely.

(Continued)

(Continued)

Sensory Construction Site

Set up the sand tray with the extra resources and encourage the children to explore freely.

Review and reflect

Encourage children to explain the type of shadows made.

- Did the window shadows look the same as, or different from, the wooden frame shadows?
- When the sunshine was bright, what did the shadows look like? When the sunshine went behind the clouds what did the shadows look like?

Encourage the children to reflect upon the materials used in the construction site.

- Did all the materials look and feel the same or different?
- What does a building site look like?
- Look at photographs or images online to prompt thinking.
- Do materials on a building site look the same or different?

Assessment

While the children are exploring building with the sensory blocks and sensory sand tray, take photographs of the children and make notes of any interesting comments to add to their learning journey records. Discuss the photographs with the children and see what they can remember about the experience.

Follow-up activities

To take the children's thinking further, opportunities can be made to introduce other 3D shapes, such as pyramids or prisms of different thickness. These can be constructed of cardboard and coloured cellophane.

ACTIVITY

Bee-Bot about Town

What you need to know

The 'Bee-Bot about Town' continuous provision activity encourages the children to freely explore operating the floor robot with links to the locality around the school or setting. If they have already been introduced to Bee-Bot, children will have a basic understanding about how to operate the floor robot and this will prompt their independent exploration.

This activity largely relates to STEM technology and mathematics through the EYFS framework-specific areas of 'Mathematics' and 'Understanding the World' via 'Technology'.

Preparation

Objectives

- To explore using technology for a purpose.
- To explore position and distance.

EYFS links

Physical development

Moving and handling - handling equipment effectively.

Personal, social and emotional development

Self-confidence and self-awareness - building confidence to try new experiences.

Making relationships - playing cooperatively, taking turns, forming positive relationships with others while playing and exploring.

Understanding the world

Technology - selecting and using technology for a purpose.

Mathematics

Shapes, spaces and measures - use of language for position and distance.

Equipment

An operational Bee-Bot is essential for this activity. Alongside the floor robot, a floor street map is needed to illustrate the local area around the school or setting. This can be constructed from large floor paper with illustrations or 3D buildings made from boxes, if possible.

Alternatively, this continuous provision activity can take place outside with a street map chalked onto the ground.

A set of floor directional cards are also helpful for warming up the children's thinking about movement and direction. These should be A4 size cards with at least five of each symbol: forwards arrow, backwards arrow, right turn and left turn.

(Continued)

(Continued)

Useful links

YouTube video about using a Bee-Bot floor robot: www.youtube.com/watch?v=52ZuenJIFyE

Setting the scene

It is important that children have already been introduced to Bee-Bot so they are aware how to operate the floor robot with basic instructions. It would also be helpful if they have been introduced to everyday language about movement and distance within mathematics.

Before this continuous provision activity starts, it would be good to share the street floor map during a group activity to clarify the representation of the area around school or setting and make links with road names in the locality.

Trigger questions

Using arrow directional cards:

- Can we arrange the floor cards into ... forwards, backwards, right, left?
- If we use one, two, three, forwards arrow cards, how many steps forwards would we take?
- If we put three backwards arrows down where would we start and where would we go?

Progress onto arrows and turns and ask the children to set the cards out and physically follow:

- If we put three forwards arrows, a right turn, then one forwards arrow where would we go? Let's try.

Time to experiment

Set up the floor map with buildings and an operational Bee-Bot to allow children to explore moving the floor robot up and down the roads on the floor map.

Review and reflect

Look at the road shapes on the map.

- Are they all straight or are some different?
- Can you describe how they look different?
- How did Bee-Bot move along the roads that were not straight?
- How did Bee-Bot move along the long roads?
- How did Bee-Bot keep on moving?

Assessment

While the children are exploring moving Bee-Bot around the floor street map, plan time to complete some short observations for their learning journey records that focus on the language they are using and their confidence in operating the Bee Bot.

Follow-up activities

To take the children's thinking further, opportunities can be taken to introduce some simple puzzle cards that add structure and specific thinking. These cards might build in a problem-solving element by asking children to programme Bee-Bot to reach a road or location on the street floor map.

ACTIVITY

Car Park Chaos!

What you need to know

The 'Car Park Chaos!' activity encourages children to manoeuvre cars and trucks in relation to corresponding numbers.

The activity largely relates to STEM mathematics through the EYFS framework-specific area of 'Mathematics'.

Preparation

Objectives

- To recognise and begin to organise numbers 1-10.
- To develop understanding about position, distance and size.

EYFS links

Physical development

Moving and handling - handling and manoeuvring cars effectively.

Personal, social and emotional development

Self-confidence and self-awareness - building confidence to try new activities.

Making relationships - playing cooperatively, taking turns, forming positive relationships with others while playing and exploring.

Mathematics

Number - counting reliably 1-20, placing in order.

Shapes, spaces and measures - use of language for position, distance and size.

(Continued)

(Continued)

Equipment

Cars or other small vehicles with number cards attached on top are essential for this activity, along with a corresponding 'car park'. A plastic, toy car park can be used or alternatively a simple car park can be constructed using a pizza box base or lid with numbered parking bays drawn on.

Useful links

Ideas for making cardboard car parks and garages can be found on Pinterest: https://uk. pinterest.com

Setting the scene

Throughout the early years, children will constantly work with the recognition and ordering of numbers. This activity relies upon children's natural mathematical curiosity. It may begin with numbers to ten but then introduce higher numbers as children's confidence and interest extends.

Trigger questions

A recap game where the children are guided to match and recognise numbers 1-10 is a good intro-duction to this activity. Examples of games could include pegging numbered cards in order on a washing line, or number snap in which children take turns at picking two cards, saying the number and keeping the cards if they match.

Questions might be:

- Which number comes before 7?
- Does 5 come before 6 or 8?
- Which number is after 4?
- Does 10 follow 9 or 5?

Time to experiment

Set up the car park and a tray of numbered vehicles. Encourage children to explore moving the vehicles around the car park and 'parking' in corresponding spaces.

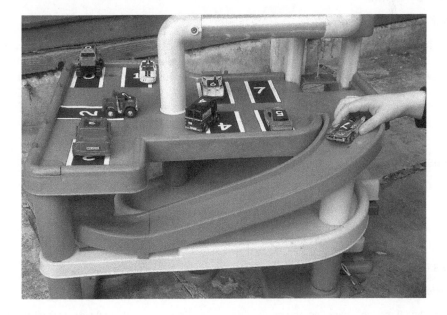

Review and reflect

- Can you park all the vehicles in order forwards and backwards?
- Can you play a game where you re-park mixed up cars?

(Continued)

(Continued)

Assessment

While the children are exploring the numbered vehicles it would be a good idea to plan some short observations focusing upon number knowledge that could be added to learning journey records and inform future teaching and learning with number recognition and ordering.

Follow-up activities

To take the children's thinking further, children should be given the opportunities to create some new numbered vehicles and corresponding new spaces within the car park. You will need extra vehicles, sticky labels such as small post-it notes, and pencils or pens.

ACTIVITY

Brick by Brick!

What you need to know

The 'Brick by Brick' activity encourages children to explore construction in the context of the real world. This activity largely relates to STEM science and mathematics through the EYFS framework-specific areas of 'Understanding the World' via 'The world' and 'Mathematics', but also has some links with design and technology via 'Expressive arts and design' and 'Exploring media and materials' and 'Being imaginative'. Through the constructive nature of this activity, there are also basic links to STEM engineering.

Preparation

Objectives

- To explore materials using tools while recognising material similarities and differences.
- To develop understanding about position, distance and size.

EYFS links

Physical development

Moving and handling – handling and manipulating Play-Doh effectively and with correct tools.

Personal, social and emotional development

Self-confidence and self-awareness – building confidence to try new activities.

Making relationships – playing cooperatively, taking turns, forming positive relationships with others while playing and exploring.

Mathematics

Shapes, spaces and measures – use of language for position, distance and exploration of everyday shapes.

Understanding the world

The world – similarities and differences related to objects and materials.

Expressive arts and design

Exploring and using media and materials – explore materials, tools and techniques.

Being imaginative – using materials in original ways, thinking about purpose.

Equipment

Wooden or plastic bricks are needed for this activity. The bigger cuboids as opposed to cube shaped bricks are better, since they are more realistic and easier for the children to build with.

Play-Doh is also needed for the children to use as 'cement' for the bricks, and tools for the Play-Doh such as rolling boards, rollers and cutters are also essential. It is best to stick to one Play-Doh colour to make this as realistic as possible and ensure there is plenty for the children to manipulate and work with.

Useful links

If you have a projector screen available in the same area the children will be building, it is often good stimulation for a loop video to play in the background. In this instance, images of bricklayers laying bricks would be good. No sound is required, just images to capture the children's interest and stimulate their thinking in an indirect way.

YouTube is very good for video clips like this. Here is one example: www.youtube.com/watch?v=sDsRhVbhNh8

Setting the scene

As part of this activity, it would be useful for the children to have had some experience of how bricks are laid. There are many short clips on YouTube that show how bricks are stacked with material in between to bind them together. Following on from this, they could begin by exploring how to roll and use Play-Doh as a substitute for cement during adult-led group time.

Trigger questions

The children may initially explore stacking the bricks without the Play-Doh. If so, encourage the children to build and then test how stable the building or tower is.

(Continued)

(Continued)

Time to experiment

Set up the bricks, Play-Doh, Play-Doh boards, rollers and cutters on a table within the same area for the children to explore and build.

Review and reflect

After the children have been exploring Play-Doh alongside the brick building for a little while, prompt thinking further:

- Think about what the Play-Doh should look like when you spread it along the brick. Should it be smooth or bumpy? Find out whether smooth or bumpy makes the bricks stick together the best.
- Can you work as a team to build a wall together? If so, how will you do this?

Assessment

While the children are exploring with building and constructing, take some photographs of their progress and add these to their learning journey records. Look for evidence that the children have a clear grasp of pattern and shapes and make a note of any mathematical language used.

Follow-up activities

To take the children's thinking further, they could be given the opportunity to add a 'design' element to the activity. This will encourage them to focus upon 'what' they would like to attempt to build first. The children can collaborate to construct a design in small groups and then work together to follow the design and construct it with the original materials.

There are numerous ways of stimulating children's mathematical and scientific thinking in the early years. The activities offered here use readily available practical materials and make links with children's daily experiences. Hopefully they will inspire you to ensure that STEM rich activities become part of your continuous provision, laying the foundations for more formal work in the primary phase.

FURTHER READING

Foundation years website: www.foundationyears.org.uk

This includes the statutory framework and a host of useful and up-to-date resources and information.

3
PRIMARY SCIENCE AND STEM

RANIA MAKLAD

SCIENCE IN THE PRIMARY SCHOOL

> Access to scientific knowledge, for peaceful purposes, from a very early age is part of the right to education belonging to all men and women ... science education is essential for human development, for creating endogenous scientific capacity and for having active and informed citizens.
>
> (UNESCO, 2000, p. 462)

It is impossible to deny the power of classroom science in creating a sense of awe and wonder as in, for example, the enthusiastic responses we receive from children every time a water balloon does not burst on top of a candle flame. Indeed, teaching science in the primary classroom has been one of the most rewarding experiences in my career; it increases children's self-confidence, improves their literacy skills and enhances their interest in STEM.

At the individual level, science enables children to make sense of the world around them, helps them develop an understanding of natural and technological phenomena, and creates curious and inquisitive minds that pose questions and seek answers. Through children's pursuit of deeper understanding of science, educators seed a love of learning that grows with their intellectual development.

The benefits of learning science from an early age apply equally to society, in that it creates a citizen base that thinks critically and analytically and is capable of making well-informed choices for their communities. As we live in an information-rich era, it is important to be able to critically evaluate societal challenges and make informed decisions - a principle that can be, at least partly, attributed to the skills learned in pursuing science education.

In developing young children's minds to think scientifically, it is important to remember that scientific knowledge is tentative and uncertain and, therefore, to focus on the development of skills to *formulate* and *assess*, rather than *acquire* knowledge. Thus, while new scientific knowledge and techniques are developed and discovered, the basic processes of scientific inquiry and evaluation remain largely constant, making *learning more of a journey than a destination.*

IN THIS CHAPTER

Some teachers find science a difficult subject to teach. This chapter introduces a number of practical activities that simplify difficult scientific concepts and outline a range of scientific inquiry skills that can be developed through hands-on experience (Dunne & Maklad, 2015).

The activities are intended to set the scene for progression in life sciences by presenting the topic of animals and their habitats from early years education (Elstgeest, 1985). Making a wormery in the classroom will help children as young as five understand the basics of living organisms. This is followed by children, from age eight years, extending their knowledge and understanding of the topic through building a bug hotel outside the classroom. The natural progression into the food chain, using owl pellets as a medium, is the final activity. These activities are presented as examples, and the literature is rich with others that can be implemented effectively to assist with science education in primary school.

ACTIVITY

Making a Wormery

What you need to know

Earthworms are essential for the wellbeing of plants. The tunnels they produce while digging in the soil change the soil structure and allow water and oxygen to enter the soil, and carbon dioxide to leave. Earthworms also mix soil layers, making it more fertile. They have an important role to play in breaking down dead organic matter (during decomposition) and they do this by digesting organic matter and breaking it down so that bacteria and fungi can feed on it and release its nutrients.

Preparation

Objectives

To know what a habitat is and to understand that living things live in habitats to which they are suited.

Curriculum links

Animals and their habitats.

Year groups

Years 1 and 2.

Equipment

Plastic jars (one per group), an elastic band, a piece of muslin cloth, sand, soil, gravel, water, grass cuttings, leaves and earthworms.

Useful links

www.earthwormsoc.org.uk

www.bbc.co.uk/nature/life/Lumbricidae#intro

Setting the scene

In class, talk about where animals live, then go on a walk around the school grounds looking for mini-beasts and their habitats. Introduce 'micro-habitat' and explain that under a wooden log might be the best home for insects like woodlice. Observe earthworms wriggling around after the rain. In small groups, ask children to think of different ways to collect earthworms without digging. Children may suggest jumping up and down, pouring water or playing music. Let the children experiment with their ideas and collect a handful of earthworms in their group's jar. If a group is unsuccessful, they can dig in their search for worms.

Trigger questions

- Have you seen earthworms before? Where did you see them?
- Do you know what environment would be suitable for worms to grow in? How can we find out?
- Do you know why earthworms are important?
- What would happen if there were no earthworms?

Time to experiment

Organise the children to work in groups of three or four and provide each group with a plastic jar. With the help of an adult, ask the children to add small stones or gravel to the bottom of the jar – explain that the stones will help with drainage. In thin layers (about a centimetre thick each), add soil then sand until the jar is nearly full. Leave enough space at the top (about 3 centimetres) to allow for the grass cuttings and leaves to be added as worm food. To keep the soil moist, add a little water but not too much otherwise the worms will not be able to breathe under the soil.

(Continued)

(Continued)

Take the children on a worm hunt; be as creative as you can. You could start a little competition between the children asking them to come up with different ways to collect worms. Children usually think of lovely ideas such as pouring water, dancing and jumping and playing music near the ground, as well as digging the top soil. Once each group has found a few worms, put them gently on top of the soil in each jar. Remind the children that earthworms are delicate and may not feel safe in children's hands. Add leaves and grass cuttings to the top of the soil. Make some small holes in the lids and screw them on the jars, before wrapping the jars with black paper. Children could use clip art and ICT to decorate the jars. Keep the jar content moist but not too wet and away from direct sun light.

Review and reflect

- Encourage the children to talk about the experience, and describe the worms and their habitat.
- Explain what was the best way to collect earthworms, and why.
- Explain the reasons behind using alternate layers of sand and soil – and the need to add gravel or stones.
- Discuss why earthworms dig deep in the soil.
- Encourage the children to reflect upon the difference and similarities of the jar and the earthworms' natural habitat.
- Consider different types of habitat and ask the children if they would be suitable for earthworms.

Assessment

The children are to observe the earthworms and find out:

- how earthworms move;
- if they breathe under the soil and how; and
- what happens to the leaves and grass cuttings at the top of the jar.

(Continued)

(Continued)

Follow-up activities

Healthy eating option: Use the wormery to encourage children to eat healthily

To feed the worms, we can offer them healthy options for lunch. Children are encouraged to bring a healthy snack and all leftovers be given to the worms. This may include banana and orange peel, apple and pear cores and bread crumbs.

Environmental option: sustainability

Use the worms to demonstrate sustainability and decomposition of biological materials. By having a composting bin in the school garden, children can observe and compare the difference in composting biological and man-made materials, e.g. crisp packets, sweets wrappers and plastic bags.

Further reading

www.earthwormsoc.org.uk

www.bbc.co.uk/nature/animals

www.earthwormsoc.org.uk/earthworm-information

ACTIVITY

Bug Hotel

What you need to know

Bug hotels - also known as bug shelters - are designed to provide a safe hideaway for wildlife. They usually add to the biodiversity of your setting but that will depend on the size and location of your bug hotel. When designing a bug hotel, you need to consider the creatures around your natural setting and/or the creatures you wish to attract; this will help you to decide whether you need to include a pond or locate the hotel in a sunny or a shady spot. Bug hotels are full of learning opportunities and they are great projects for the children to be involved in and learn about their natural environment.

Preparation

Objectives

To know what a habitat is and to understand that living things live in habitats to which they are suited.

Curriculum links

Living things and their habitats.

Year groups

Years 1 to 6, depending on the resources used to build the bug hotel.

Equipment

The following is not an exhaustive list of the materials needed to create a bug hotel but may provide inspiration: wooden pallets, flowerpots, dead wood, logs, branches and twigs, hollow pipes, tubes and bamboo canes, dry leaves, loose bark, waterproof signs/pictures and magnifying glasses.

Setting the scene

Where do mini-beasts live? Insects need a safe place – like a bug hotel – to live in. A bug hotel will provide an opportunity for the children to investigate and discover different insects and their habitats. Arrange for the materials chosen by you and the children to be available in an area designated for a bug hotel. Remind the children to bring old clothes and possibly gloves. It would be useful to invite parents or members of the community to help the children build the bug hotel.

Trigger questions

Explain that the bug hotel will need to have 'rooms' that are exactly right for the mini-beast guests. The features of each habitat within the bug hotel need to be suited to the bugs. You can ask the question:

- Do all insects live in the same environment?

Time to experiment

Following on from the wormery in the glass jar, start by discussing the idea of building a bigger place for the worms and other bugs to live in. Invertebrates like cool damp conditions, so a semi-shaded area, by a hedge or under a big tree, might be a good place for a bug hotel.

Pile the wooden pallets on top of each other to create a tier effect (see picture below) – four or five levels would be a good and safe height. Fill in the gaps with other materials: dead wood is great for wood boring beetles; hollow stems and canes are ideal for bees; stone and tiles provide a cool moist place for frogs and newts; dry leaves are brilliant for ladybirds.

(Continued)

(Continued)

In a dry place, close to the bug hotel, or in a topic corner of the classroom, keep insect identification sheets and some magnifying glasses for the children to explore the bug hotel.

Review and reflect

- What insects can the children find in and around the bug hotel?
- Can the children name these insects?
- Can they describe the insects and use comparative language?
- Are they able to link the insects to their habitats?
- Do they understand the role insects play in our eco-system?

Assessment

Using the identification sheets and magnifying glasses, can the children recognise some common insects? Can they identify their body parts and explain their contribution to the environment? Will the bugs stay all year round? For what reasons might they leave (e.g. too cold, too hot, not enough food)? In what ways will the bug hotel change during the year? How will the features of each of the microhabitats change (e.g. at night, in the summer, when it rains)?

Follow-up activities

Food chain

Use the bug hotel to help children understand the place of mini-beasts in the food chain. Insects are underestimated for their role in the food chain. They are the only food to many amphibians, reptiles, birds and mammals. Without insects to help breakdown dead animals and plants the world would be a very messy place.

Owl pellet

To develop the theme of interdependence, observe and investigate owl pellets to find evidence of the food chain process and the part played by the barn owl.

Further reading

https://ypte.org.uk

www.edenproject.com

Websites

www.earthwormsoc.org.uk

www.bbc.co.uk/nature/life/Lumbricidae#intro

www.wildaboutgardens.org.uk/thingstodo/inaweekend/bug-mansion.aspx

www.inspirationgreen.com/insect-habitats.html

https://schoolgardening.rhs.org.uk/Resources/Project/Make-a-bug-hotel

ACTIVITY

Food Chain

What you need to know

All living things need energy to live, grow, move and reproduce. The main source of energy for animals and humans is food, while plants get their energy through photosynthesis. The food chain is a simple way to demonstrate how each living thing acquires energy and how nutrients and energy are passed from one living thing to another. All food chains start with plant life and end with animal life. In the food chain, plants are called producers because they produce their own food, while animals are called consumers as they eat plants and other animals and do not make their own food. Animals are divided into three groups: herbivores that eat plants only, carnivores that eat animals only, and omnivores (including humans), which eat both plants and other animals. Animals that eat other animals are called predators, and the animals they eat are called prey.

In the food chain, we also have decomposers – primarily bacteria and fungi that help break down decaying matter like dead plants and animals, and release the nutrients in their bodies into the environment. With these nutrients (plus water and sun) helping plants to grow, the full cycle of life and energy can be completed.

Food chains explain how plants, animals and humans depend on each other for food. The main three sections of the food chains are:

1. Animals and plants are linked by food chains.
2. Producers and consumers.
3. Prey and predators.

It is important to emphasise that if one part of the food chain alters, the whole chain is affected.

A simple food chain can start with grass that is eaten by a rabbit. Then the rabbit is eaten by the fox.

A bigger food chain will include more animals. For example, grass, insect, frog, snake and then an eagle.

(Continued)

(Continued)

Preparation

Objectives

To construct and interpret a variety of food chains, identifying producers, predators and prey.

Curriculum links

Animals, including humans; life cycles; food chains.

Year groups

Years 4, 5 and 6.

Equipment

Owl pellets can be ordered from several internet sites. Try to choose a British source, e.g. the Barn Owl Trust, as this will give the children a better understanding of the British eco-system. As well as pellets, you need plastic tweezers, cocktail sticks, a small pot for soaking the pellets, a few drops of clear antiseptic or disinfectant, some sheets of newspaper, a hand lens, a shallow dish on which to dissect the pellets and gloves to wear when handling and dissecting the pellets.

Setting the scene

What are pellets? Explain that most birds produce pellets. Pellets are small objects containing the birds' undigested food that is regurgitated (through the mouth). They consist of things like bones, teeth and claws and are usually enclosed by softer materials like fur.

Owls often swallow their prey completely, passing through the gizzard prior to entering the stomach. The solid remains are prevented from passing any further through the digestive system and squeezed in the gizzard. Owls regurgitate these pellets twice a day.

Studying pellets gives us a great deal of information about owls' eating habits, which in turn teaches us about food chains and the owls' part in them.

Trigger questions

- Where do we get our energy from?
- Where do animals get their energy from – and what about plants?
- What happens to animals and plants when they die?
- What is owls' favourite food?
- What do mushrooms live on?

Time to experiment

Pellets can be torn apart when dry, but it is best to use a sprayer with a little disinfected water. Tear each pellet apart very carefully using plastic tweezers and cocktail sticks. Search carefully as you go so that nothing is missed. As you find bones or other items, remove them from the pellet, clean them and place them on sheets of newspaper to dry. Take note of the basic materials in the pellet. Is it mainly fur or feathers, or something else? Would you expect to find the skeleton of a small bird or mammal?

Review and reflect

Once the children have identified the contents of pellets, they can answer the following questions:

- When do owls hunt? Some mammals are active during both day and night, but others only hunt at night.
- Where do owls hunt? Some creatures prefer grassland to woods and hedges.
- How much do owls eat?
- What part do owls play in the food chain?

Assessment

It is recommended for each group of children to have a piece of card with their names and the date written clearly. The children are to list the materials found in the pellet on the card and stick the materials on the card with strong glue. Teachers can use the identification cards available on the Barn Owl Trust website and ask the children to write the name of the animal from which the pellet material came. Once the card has fully dried and been suitably labelled, children can keep it in a suitable polythene bag. Beyond this activity, teachers are encouraged to explore the many worksheet and display ideas to help children improve their understanding of food chains.

Follow-up activities

To follow up on food chains, children could investigate the life cycles of various creatures and compare the life cycles of a mammal, an amphibian, an insect and a bird. Having a caterpillar in the classroom is a cheap and valuable resource. It also helps to correct many misconceptions the children have from reading fiction stories about caterpillars and butterflies. For example, caterpillars will only eat green leaves contrary to the story where it eats cake, sausages and ice-cream. Depending on the type of the caterpillar, it takes between a week or two to hatch into a butterfly. This is also different from The Hungry Caterpillar story the children are familiar with.

REFERENCES

Dunne, M. & Maklad, R. (2015) Doing science. In M. Dunne & A. Peacock (ed.), *Primary Science: A Guide to Teaching Practice*. London: Sage, pp. 47–68.

Elstgeest, J. (1985) The right question at the right time. In W. Harlen (ed.), *Primary Science: Talking in the Plunge*. London: Heinemann, pp. 36–46.

UNESCO. (2000) *Science for the Twenty-First Century: A New Commitment*. Proceedings of World Conference on Science, Budapest, 26 June to 1 July 1999. Paris: UNESCO. Available at http://unesdoc.unesco.org/images/0012/001207/120706e.pdf (accessed 20 April 2017).

WEBSITES

Animated food chain game: www.brainpop.co.uk/games/foodchaingame

BBC Bitesize – Food chains: www.bbc.co.uk/education/topics/zbhhvcw

BBC Bitesize – What is a food chain?: www.bbc.co.uk/guides/z3c2xnb

The Barn Owl Trust: www.barnowltrust.org.uk

4

MATHEMATICS IN STEM EDUCATION

SUE POPE

Mathematics is essential to the communication and understanding of STEM ideas. It provides a powerful means of manipulating data and quantitative information and is a truly universal language. Mathematics is a notoriously difficult subject both to learn and to teach. The purpose of mathematics in school is manifold; most importantly it is about developing ways of thinking that will be important throughout life. Ideally, children acquire an 'at homeness' with number that allows them to estimate with confidence, make choices about the mathematics to use when tackling problems and critique numerical and graphical representations of information. In addition, mathematics is subject to frequent high stakes testing, which can distort teaching and learning as children are 'taught to the test'. Skemp (1976) introduced the notions of instrumental and relational understanding: instrumental is being able to do something without understanding why. Relational understanding is both know how and know why, it is more powerful as it enables children to use their mathematics in a variety of contexts. Haylock (2010) says the most important thing that children can gain from mathematics in the primary school is 'they learn how to learn mathematics'.

While mathematics is essential to STEM education, it is also so much more than STEM. Mathematics is used in personal finance, business and commerce, accountancy, economics, logistics and social sciences. Many disciplines make extensive use of statistics to analyse data and make sense of the information so readily available in modern society. Mathematics is also an important discipline in its own right, beautiful and powerful, with a rich cultural and historical heritage. Learning experiences that combine mathematics with other subjects expose its power as an essential tool.

When using mathematics across the curriculum it is important to consider the learning purposes. While there might sometimes be good reason why you want children to work without technological aids for calculating or manipulating data, in the vast majority of cases these will be essential if meaningful work is to be undertaken in STEM education. The manipulation and presentation of real data is so much easier with a spreadsheet, which can also undertake calculations quickly and accurately. That way, arithmetic does not get in the way of mathematical and scientific thinking.

IN THIS CHAPTER

The activities in this chapter are intended to illustrate ways of using and developing mathematical understanding through STEM learning experiences. It is possible to exploit opportunities for developing essential mathematical skills across the curriculum by adapting some of the ideas presented here. The ASE guide on *The Language of Mathematics in Science* is a valuable source for mathematical and scientific conventions (ASE, 2016).

ESSENTIAL MATHEMATICAL SKILLS

The activities in this chapter will help children to develop and use the mathematical skills listed below. For more on these mathematical skills see Haylock (2010).

- The importance of mental methods as a first resort, and interpretation of calculator/spreadsheet outputs - what to do with all the digits? (rounding/levels of accuracy)

- How to measure accurately distance, time, mass, capacity, etc.

- How to use a spreadsheet to record, manipulate and represent data. This includes using simple formulae.

- How to represent data - which charts are appropriate/suitable for different types of data and how some charts can be misleading (e.g. 3D bar charts and pie charts).

- How to summarise data - the mean, median and mode can be found with a simple command on a spreadsheet - children need to understand the limitations of each of these measures of central tendency.

ACTIVITY

Whose Paper Aeroplane Is Best?

What you need to know

This practical, experimental activity allows children to be creative in designing or selecting a paper aeroplane and devising a fair test to determine the 'best' paper aeroplane. Children can collect and analyse their experimental data in a spreadsheet, which allows them to explore different ways of analysing their data.

Preparation

Objectives

Work cooperatively to devise and implement a fair test to determine the best paper aeroplane.

Curriculum links

Design and technology: designing and making paper aeroplanes.

Science: working scientifically – designing a fair test and agreeing the criteria for 'best'.

Mathematics: measuring distance and time accurately, calculating mean and representing data.

Computing: use of spreadsheets.

Year groups

Suitable for Years 4, 5 and 6.

Equipment

Paper (recycled paper is perfectly good for making paper aeroplanes), metre rules, tape measures, timing device (stop watch, smart phone, etc.), use of spreadsheets to record and represent data. You may well need to use the school hall for the practical experiments, as conducting experiments outdoors may lead to spurious results if there is any wind.

Useful links

There are numerous websites that have instructions for paper aeroplanes and most have background information, including videos. For example:

www.paperaeroplanes.com

www.origami-resource-center.com/paper-airplane-instructions.html

http://eng.origami-kids.com/paper-airplane

Setting the scene

There are many ways you could introduce this activity. You could ask students to research paper aeroplanes for homework and to bring in ones they have made. Alternatively, you could bring in an example, fly it across the classroom and ask if they can make a better aeroplane. Or you could start with a short video (e.g. the Origami Kids website shows different types of paper aeroplanes in action).

Children should work in groups to decide what criteria they are going to use and how they will conduct a fair test to determine 'the best paper aeroplane'. There is no 'correct' way to do this. Children need to be encouraged to justify their decisions and work towards making a presentation to the rest of the class about their work.

(Continued)

(Continued)

Trigger questions

- What makes a good paper aeroplane?
- Do you need to use someone else's design?
- Does it matter what size and type of paper is used to make the aeroplane?
- What features of the aeroplane make it fly faster/further/higher/longer?
- How will you ensure your test is fair?
- What data will you record? How?

Time to experiment

Which paper aeroplane is best? In your group, agree how you will answer this question.

Will you design your own aeroplane or try different aeroplanes that others have designed?

What data will you collect? How will you ensure the data have been fairly collected?

How will you present your findings?

Review and reflect

- How fair was the test you applied?
- Could someone else reproduce your results?
- Is there any other data you could have collected?
- Could you have presented your results differently?
- Having seen how other groups tackled the question – how might you change what you did?
- How well did your group work together?

Assessment

It is worth negotiating with children in advance of the presentations, what they think will make a good presentation for this activity. They can then use those criteria to self-assess their own approach and apply them to the other presentations.

What have they learned about working on an activity like this together?

Follow-up activities

Having shared results from each group, children may want to adapt their approach and look for another 'best' aeroplane. Alternatively, they may want to work as a class to identify the 'best' aeroplane by devising a fair test for the 'best' aeroplane from each group.

Children could examine the design of the 'best' aeroplanes and try to design a superior aeroplane, drawing on their experimental results.

Children may want to research the history of flight and how aeroplanes work.

ACTIVITY

Use of Water

What you need to know

This activity exposes children to an important global social issue – access to and use of clean water. It gives children the opportunity to appreciate how something they probably take for granted is a precious resource for others in the world. They can also start to consider the impact of choices they make and simple ways in which they can help to save water.

Preparation

Objectives

Use of mathematics to compare the use of water in different parts of the world.

Curriculum links

Science: the importance of water for life.

Mathematics: measuring and estimating capacity.

Computing: use of spreadsheets to record data.

Year groups

This activity can be accessible to children of any age depending on the approach taken. Use of Gapminder and Bowland Maths Mellow Yellow would be more suitable for Years 5 and 6.

Equipment

Measuring jugs, buckets.

Useful links

There are many useful sources for work on this topic.

Modern water systems: www.bbc.co.uk/programmes/p0114f7c

Access to water in other countries; there are many charities that have information, e.g. The Water Project: https://thewaterproject.org/why-water/

Water Aid: www.wateraid.org/uk

You can also use Gapminder to visualise the data: www.gapminder.org/data/

Bowland Maths Mellow Yellow part of You Reckon resource: www.bowlandmaths.org.uk/materials/projects/online/you_reckon/You%20Reckon_Web/page_06.htm

(Continued)

(Continued)

Setting the scene

You could start by asking children what they use water for in their everyday lives (e.g. drinking, preparing food, washing, flushing the toilet, cleaning). They could work in small groups to capture their ideas in words and pictures on a large piece of paper. A whole class discussion could follow looking at the different groups' ideas – why is water important to human life?

Ask the children if they have ever been to/lived in another country – could they drink water directly from the tap? Were there any restrictions on the use of water? Watch a video about how water is processed in modern society so we have drinking quality water from our taps. Use images/video to show what happens in other countries, e.g. Western countries where water is scarce – desalination, bottled water, save water schemes such as California's Mellow Yellow.

Trigger questions

- How much water do you use every day?
- What do you use water for?
- How much water do children in other countries use?
- Why does water use vary across the world?
- If you only had one bucket of water a day what would you prioritise?

Time to experiment

Collect data about how much water you use each day by keeping a water diary for a week. Estimate how much water is used for different activities (e.g. showering for five or ten minutes, having a bath, cleaning your teeth – with the tap running or not?, flushing the toilet, drinking).

Use a spreadsheet to record your results and find an average daily amount. How does your water use compare with other people's? Are there ways you could save water? The results for the class could be collated and children can discuss the variation in the data (i.e. why some people use more water than others). Are there ways we could all save water? Children could work in groups to produce posters about the ways in which water could be saved.

Review and reflect

- How accurate was your water diary?
- Why does water use differ across the world?
- In what ways can we save water?
- How well did your group work together?

Assessment

What have they learned about themselves as users of water?

What have they learned about working together on an activity like this together?

Follow-up activities

How much does water cost? Investigate the difference between water rates and having a water meter. How could people save money on water costs?

ACTIVITY

Modelling the Solar System

What you need to know

This activity uses a context likely to be fascinating for children to help them learn about the planets in our solar system and manipulate related numerical information. The information provided will need to be adapted depending on the age of the children. Younger children may simply order the planets relative to the Sun and instruct a programmable toy to travel to different planets, whereas older children might work with scale and find different ways of ordering the planets.

Preparation

Objectives

Work co-operatively to create a scaled representation of the distances of planets in the solar system from the Earth.

Curriculum links

Science: understanding the solar system.

Mathematics: measuring distance accurately, use of scale.

Computing: use of programmable robots/floor turtles.

Year groups

This activity can be used with all children, with suitable modification, e.g. Years 1 and 2 could order the planets and instruct a programmable toy (e.g. Bee-Bot) to travel between them; in Years 5 and 6 children could work with scale and different units.

Equipment

Metre rules, tape measures, trundle wheel, pictures of the planets, for each group an information sheet about the planets in the solar system and a set of pictures.

(Continued)

(Continued)

Useful links

There are some stunning videos of the solar system. Useful background is available at www.kids astronomy.com/solar_system.htm

The planets in order of size can be viewed at www.solarsystemquick.com/planets-scale-of-size.htm

Planet facts

Body	Equatorial radius	Distance from the Sun		Period of orbit	
	km	millions km	AU*	days	years
Sun	695,500	-		-	-
Earth	6,378	149.6	1.0	365.26	1
Jupiter	71,492	778.41	5.2	4,332.82	11.9
Mars	3,397	227.94	1.5	686.98	1.9
Mercury	2,440	57.91	0.4	87.97	0.2
Neptune	24,764	4,498.25	30.1	60,190.03	164.8
Saturn	60,268	1,426.73	9.5	10,755.7	29.5
Uranus	25,559	2,870.97	19.2	30,687.15	84
Venus	6,052	108.21	0.7	224.7	0.6

* Astronomical units, where the distance from the Earth to the Sun is 1.

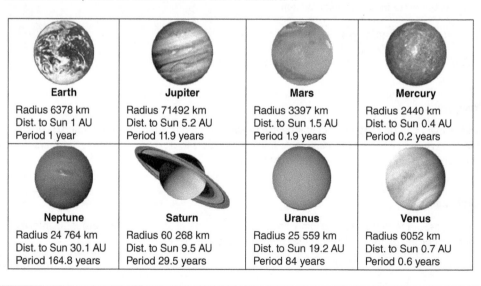

Earth	Jupiter	Mars	Mercury
Radius 6378 km	Radius 71492 km	Radius 3397 km	Radius 2440 km
Dist. to Sun 1 AU	Dist. to Sun 5.2 AU	Dist. to Sun 1.5 AU	Dist. to Sun 0.4 AU
Period 1 year	Period 11.9 years	Period 1.9 years	Period 0.2 years

Neptune	Saturn	Uranus	Venus
Radius 24 764 km	Radius 60 268 km	Radius 25 559 km	Radius 6052 km
Dist. to Sun 30.1 AU	Dist. to Sun 9.5 AU	Dist. to Sun 19.2 AU	Dist. to Sun 0.7 AU
Period 164.8 years	Period 29.5 years	Period 84 years	Period 0.6 years

Setting the scene

It is worth asking the children what they know about the solar system. Depending on their age they may know very little but they will have heard of the Sun, the Earth and the Moon and it is worth showing them a picture as they identify them. Older children may have heard of Mars and Venus. Ask how big are they? How far away are they? Then try other names and pictures.

In groups, arrange the pictures of the planets in order of distance from the Sun. Depending on the age of the children they could work out the distances between the planets in their groups or you could ask groups to work out one or two distances. Collate the information as a class and discuss how the information could be represented on a piece of paper, on the floor or wall of the classroom or in the playground, so that the relative distances could be appreciated. This will raise the need for scale.

Trigger questions

- Why are all the distances given from the Sun?
- Which planets are closest to Earth?
- Can you put the planets in order of distance from the Sun?
- Can you put the planets in order of size?
- Can you put the planets in order of mass?
- Is the Moon a planet?
- Do other planets have moons?
- How do planets move?
- How long does it take for each planet to orbit the Sun?

Time to experiment

In groups, arrange the pictures of the planets in different orders, such as by mass, radius or period. As before, depending on the age of the children they could work out the distances between the planets in their groups or you could ask groups to work out just one or two distances. Collate the information as a class and discuss how the information could be represented on a piece of paper, on the floor or wall of the classroom or in the playground, so that the relative distances could be appreciated. This will raise the need for scale.

In the playground, a representation will allow children to physically travel between the different planets and the Sun and experience for themselves the relative difference in distance between the planets.

In the classroom, a (scaled) representation on the floor can be used as a track for programmable robots/floor turtles.

Small groups could research a particular planet and make a poster to display their findings. This will provide an attractive classroom display. Are the planets ever lined up like this? Could they ever be?

Review and reflect

- What have you learned about the solar system?
- How did you choose what to include in your poster?

(Continued)

(Continued)

- What mathematics have you used?
- How well did your group work together?

Assessment

It is worth negotiating with children in advance what sort of information should be included to make a good poster. They can then use those criteria to self-assess their poster and apply them to the other posters.

What have they learned about working together?

Follow-up activities

Investigating the orbit periods and the paths followed by planets is a good extension for older children.

These activities illustrate some of the exciting ways that mathematics can be used across the curriculum, to engage learners and develop scientific thinking and understanding.

REFERENCES

ASE. (2016) *The Language of Mathematics in Science*. Available at www.ase.org.uk/resources/maths-in-science.

Haylock, D. (2010) *Mathematics Explained for Primary Teachers*. London: Sage.

Skemp, R. R. (1976) Relational understanding and instrumental understanding. *Mathematics Teaching*, 77(1), 20–26.

FURTHER READING

Cross, A. & Borthwick, A. (2016) *Connecting Primary Maths and Science*. London: Open University Press.

Hansen, A. & Vaukins, D. (2011) *Primary Mathematics across the Curriculum*. Exeter: Learning Matters.

5
DESIGN AND TECHNOLOGY IN STEM

BEN SEDMAN AND ANNE GUILFORD

Design and technology (D&T) is essential to the communication and understanding of STEM ideas, and is the school subject closest to engineering. Content within D&T relies heavily on science and mathematics. The use of scientific and mathematical concepts and principles, when designing and making products, provides meaning and relevance to children.

D&T is the only practical, hands-on, technical subject taught in schools. It plays an important role in providing children with imaginative, creative experiences, and develops a practical identity and a capability for innovation. The subject introduces children to the knowledge and skills required for creative design, innovation and engineering, essential for STEM. Children are encouraged to solve problems, a key life skill, and through this, learn to complete activities without all the necessary information. Undertaking such activities empowers learners and develops their self-confidence.

Finally, the subject provides opportunities to develop a range of transferable skills, including collaboration, team working and communication, all of which are essential for future employment within the STEM sector.

At the heart of all design and technology projects must be the *designing*, *making* and *evaluating* process. When designing, it is essential for learners to consider the potential users, the purpose and functionality of their products. They should be encouraged to make innovative and authentic design decisions.

Design technology allows children to design, make and evaluate products using a broad range of materials and components, for example, construction materials, textiles, food, mechanical components and electrical components. The principles of nutrition and healthy eating are readily explored through D&T with children learning how to prepare and cook a variety of dishes.

When planning D&T projects it is important to include the following phases:

1.   Investigative and evaluative activities where children can examine existing products.

2.   Focused activities where the children develop practical skills relevant to the project.

3.   Design, make and evaluate activities where children are challenged to make a product.

IN THIS CHAPTER

This chapter introduces practical activities with real world relevance that challenge children to design, make and evaluate using materials such as wood, plastic and fabric. They explore features of D&T such as wood working techniques, mechanical and electrical systems, and food technology. There are links with a range of skills, including precise measuring, CAD design, 3D printing, photography and sewing, together with opportunities to develop technical vocabulary. Children take objects apart to find out how they are made, and each activity emphasises reflection and evaluation as part of the design process.

ACTIVITY

Mechanisms: Design and Make a Controllable Vehicle

What you need to know

Phase 1: evaluate and dissemble existing products - evaluate a range of toy vehicles.

Phase 2: children learn how to add an axle to a jinks frame.

Phase 3: set the challenge to design and make a moving vehicle using a jinks frame.

A *jinks frame* is a wooden rectangle created using four pieces of 10 mm square section timber and eight cardboard triangles.

For this activity, children will need to be able to measure using a ruler. Measuring skills could be developed during a mathematics lesson. Teachers will be required to demonstrate using tools safely. Children should be introduced to different cutting equipment, such as saws, from an early age.

Preparation

Objective

Create a jinks frame to make a moving vehicle.

Curriculum links

D&T: design, make and evaluate; mechanical systems; electrical systems.

Mathematics: perimeter and area, shape and space, measures (lengths).

ICT: Google SketchUp (3D Design), 3D printing (creating a chassis and axle).

Year groups

Suitable for Years 3, 4, 5 and 6. Older children might use 3D printing to make the jinks frame.

Equipment

Dowel rods, 10 mm square section timber, bench hook, junior hacksaw, PVA glue, card triangles, wood or card wheels, mitre block, sand paper, lynx jointers, squared paper, card, motor, batteries, LEDs, buzzers, elastic bands, motors.

Useful links

Design and Technology Association: www.data.org.uk/for-education/primary

Setting the scene

Discuss and evaluate a range of different moving vehicles (products). Children could bring in toy vehicles from home. Ensure technical vocabulary (e.g. axles, chassis, wheels) is developed and children understand how a moving vehicle works.

Possible activities:

- A Venn diagram sorting activity (link to mathematics). Sort vehicles with fixed or moving axles. This could be carried out on large sheets of paper or in the hall with plastic hoops if you want to physically place the toy vehicles in each section.
- Sit in a circle and pass round a toy vehicle. Each child takes it in turn to describe a feature. The teacher could write up new technical vocabulary as it arises.
- Sketch and label parts of a moving vehicle. Annotated diagrams, cross sections and exploded diagrams could be used.
- Research vehicles on the internet.
- Go on a vehicle walk. Photograph different types of vehicles found in the local area. Discuss the moving parts and mechanisms.

Trigger questions

- What different types of vehicles can you think of?
- Why are vehicles important?
- What do we use vehicles for?
- What moving parts are there?

(Continued)

(Continued)

- What mechanisms have been included in the design?
- What materials have been used to make the vehicle?
- How have vehicles evolved over time?
- How might vehicles look in the future?
- How might you change the design to make it more appealing/function better?

Time to experiment

Complete some teacher-led focused activities to support the development of the children's knowledge, understanding and practical capabilities. For example, the teacher might demonstrate:

- How to create a jinks frame.
- How to join the axles and wheels to a jinks frame.
- How to connect a battery pack and motor to a jinks frame.

Design, make and evaluate assignment (DMEA)

Challenge the children to design, make and evaluate a controllable vehicle.

1) A jinks frame is the chassis for your vehicle. Measure four sides for your jinks frame from a piece of 10 mm square section timber. Draw the jinks frame (a square or rectangle) on centimetre squared paper.

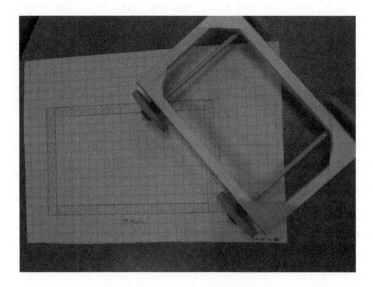

2) Indicate the length of each of the four sides of the jinks frame. It might be useful to colour each side a different colour; this will help when measuring the sides.

3) Cut out the four pieces of 10 mm square section timber that will make the jinks frame. Place each piece of square section timber on top of the plan on the square paper to check each piece is the correct size.

It might be useful to have a teaching resource like this for the children to refer to. It demonstrates the steps taken to create a jinks frame.

A jinks frame could be used to make a picture frame or the side of a building.

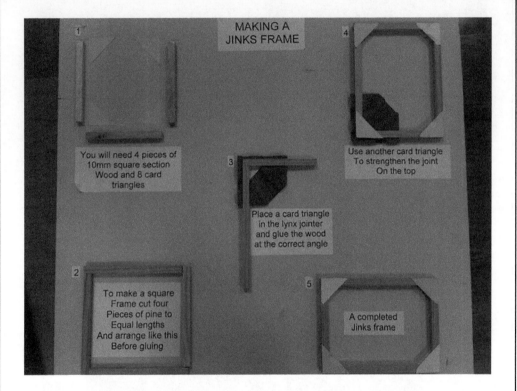

4) Stick the corners together using the card triangles and a lynx jointer. Lynx jointers hold the corners in place. This is useful when working with younger children. Just put glue on two sides of the card triangle and place it on the timber join. There is no need to glue the timber directly.

5) Once the jinks frame has been completed, add the wheels and axles to the frame. Use card axle holders to support the axles.

6) The image below shows a finished jinks frame (vehicle chassis) with axles and wheels. You can add wheel stoppers if desired.

7) Show the children a circuit diagram for a motor. Demonstrate how this could be placed in the car and discuss how a switch could be used and why this might be useful.

(Continued)

(Continued)

8) Children add a battery and motor to their vehicle, then test it works.

9) Now create the seat or cabin for your vehicle. Discuss the appearance and finishing techniques. Could recycled materials be incorporated?

You could create a net for an open card box or use recycled materials. This could be linked to different topics, e.g. design and make a Roman chariot or a moon buggy.

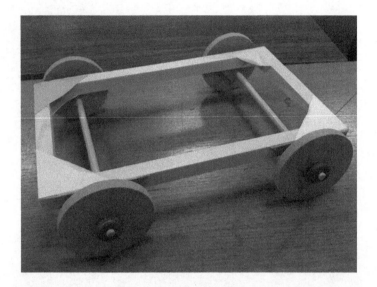

(Continued)

(Continued)

Review and reflect

Evaluate the functionality of the vehicles:

- Does the vehicle fit the design brief?
- If repeating this activity, what modifications would be made?
- Did the materials chosen support the construction of the product?
- What key technical language has been acquired?
- What has been learned?

Assessment

Children could sell their product back to the rest of the class, *Dragons' Den*-style. Discuss what makes their design special. Why do the materials they have used work well? What features do their vehicles include?

Use two stars and a wish for peer evaluation. Discuss the materials used and the joining and finishing techniques.

Use role play to hot seat an astronaut or a Roman soldier. What do they like about their moon buggy or chariot? How could the design be improved?

Follow-up activities

Add different components such as LEDs and buzzers. Test a range of waterproof materials that could be used to protect their vehicle from the rain.

Use 3D printing to create a jinks frame, wheels or an axle. See www.facebook.com/toyfabb

ACTIVITY

Design, Make and Evaluate a Pencil Case

What you need to know

Use a variety of textiles to create an innovative product, a pencil case, that matches the intended purpose. Ensure the product is functional and not just decorative. Choose fabric carefully. For example, felt is easier to use. Make sure that fabrics are cut ready and in manageable sizes. Children will need a basic understanding of threading needles and stitching. Ensure children are not just gluing different parts of their design together. You could ask a local designer to speak to the children to inspire them and discuss their work. Children could research textile work created by their favourite designers.

Preparation

Objective

Design, make and evaluate a pencil case using textiles and different stitching techniques.

Curriculum links

Design and technology: design, make and evaluate; use of textiles.

Science: materials and their properties.

ICT: CAD & digital cameras.

Mathematics: measures.

Art and design: investigate patterns and colours.

English: report writing; persuasive language.

Year groups

Suitable for children from Year 2 and above. Older children might use a sewing machine, or more sophisticated fastenings.

Equipment

Needles, thread, pins, pinking shears, textile scissors, felt, recycled textiles, computers, fasteners (toggles, press studs, buttons, Velcro, etc.).

Useful links

www.wikihow.com/Make-a-Pencil-Case

http://sewing.about.com/od/techniques/tp/handsewing.htm

www.pinterest.com/pin/201184308328743335/

www.bbc.co.uk/education/topics/zcwdmp3/resources/1

Setting the scene

Introduce children to a range of pencil cases created from different materials, for example, wood, plastic and textiles. Discuss the different design features and the functionality of each design. Disassemble one to find out how it has been put together. Think about what stitching techniques have been used.

Children could search the web to find examples or bring a pencil case in from home to share with the class. The teacher can show examples of finished pencil cases created by other children.

(Continued)

(Continued)

Trigger questions

- What materials have been used in the design?
- What joining techniques have been included (e.g. stitches, glue)?
- Who has the pencil case been designed for (e.g. children, adults)?

- What fasteners have been incorporated? How have they been joined to the materials?
- Is the design appealing? How might you improve the design?

Time to experiment

First complete some teacher-led focused activities to support the development of the children's knowledge, understanding and practical capabilities. For example, the teacher might demonstrate:

- How to thread a needle (a variety of needle and thread sizes can be used). Demonstrate how to start and stop sewing.
- How to use different stitching techniques, e.g. running stitch, backstitch and more complex chain and satin stitches.
- How to investigate different ways to attach fasteners, e.g. zips, ties, clasps, buttons, Velcro, press studs and toggles) to materials.
- How to use computer-aided-design (CAD) when designing the pencil case.

Next, challenge the children to *design*, *make* and *evaluate* a pencil case using textiles and fasteners. Felt is an easier textile to work with, but you could use recycled textiles. Children could photograph the different stages of their work and upload it to a class blog. Digital cameras could be used to take photographs that will enable digital fabric printing to be incorporated in the designs.

The challenge can follow these steps:

- In pairs or individually, plan the initial design on paper, on a mood board or using CAD. Decide on the audience for the pencil case. Children can research ideas through market research or search designs on the internet. Some children might need templates.
- Ask children to list the materials and tools they will use, including fastenings and any recycled resources.
- Using felt (and/or recycled materials) create pencil cases. Encourage the children to use a variety of stitching techniques, which can be differentiated according to age.
- Review and evaluate practical work throughout. Question the choices of materials, fasteners and stitching used.

Review and reflect

Discuss whether your stitching techniques were effective.

- Does your pencil case close?
- Why did you choose your particular design?
- Does your finished product look like your initial design?
- How could you improve your design further?

(Continued)

(Continued)

- What would you do differently if you were to repeat this activity?
- Is the design appealing?
- How might you improve the design?

Assessment

Encourage children to assess each other's completed pencil cases. Did they use different stitching techniques? How well does the pencil case close? Does the pencil case function correctly? Suggest ways the designs could be improved.

Follow-up activities

Design a package for your pencil case. Include persuasive language to catch potential customers' attention.

Add a simple electronic circuit and LED lights to brighten up your pencil case. You could also experiment with electronic paint! www.bareconductive.com/shop/electric-paint-10ml/

ACTIVITY

Design and Make a Light Source

What you need to know

Children will design and make a light source with an electrical circuit and a switch. This will support the electricity topic taught in science. A circuit is a path through which electricity passes. Electrical engineering includes the study of electricity and the design of electrical systems such as circuits and computer chips. Electrical engineers work in electronics, telecommunications and control systems.

The definition of a light source could include a traditional torch, a night lamp, a lantern or a table decoration. The topic could be linked to festivals (Christmas, Diwali and Hanukkah). You could refer to the Olympic torch, the torch held by the Statue of Liberty and discuss what they represent.

Make sure the bulbs and batteries match, e.g. 1.5v bulb with a 1.5v battery. Check the condition of the batteries and bulbs prior to the lessons. Highlight health and safety issues.

Preparation

Objective

Create a light source that has a visible switch to turn the bulb on or off with the circuit hidden from sight.

Curriculum links

Design and technology: design, make and evaluate; electrical systems.

Science: electricity.

Mathematics: measures.

ICT: CAD, QR Codes, Blogs and iMovie.

English: script writing for an advert.

RE: link to festivals of light.

Year groups

Suitable for children in Years 4, 5 and 6. Older children could investigate different types of switch and remote controls (see follow-up activity).

Equipment

Bulbs, bulb holder, crocodile clips, card, paper fasteners, foil, paperclips, battery pack, batteries, variety of switches, variety of torches.

Useful links

www.bbc.co.uk/education/topics/zq99q6f/resources/1

www.bbc.co.uk/education/topics/zjxmn39/resources/1

http://technologytom.com/html/torches.html

Setting the scene

Discuss why we use light sources or torches in everyday life. Have a collection of old and new torch designs (children could bring in a torch from home – one their parents or grandparents used). This could be set up as a timeline.

Children could investigate and evaluate designs, referring to:

- Materials used (metal, plastic)
- Size and shape of the torch (purpose)
- Shape and size of battery
- Size and shape of switch

Prepare a variety of different light source designs for children to investigate and evaluate.

(Continued)

(Continued)

Trigger questions

- What sort of light source shall I design?

- Who shall I make it for? What parts will it have?

- How will it appeal to the user?

- How will I incorporate a switch within my design?

- Which switch design will be suitable for my design?

- What materials will I need to make the light source?

- How will I ensure the circuit is not visible?

Time to experiment

Focused activities:

- Ask the children to create a handmade switch choosing from card, foil, paper fasteners, paperclips. Once they have experimented, demonstrate some designs to ensure all are able to create a simple switch.

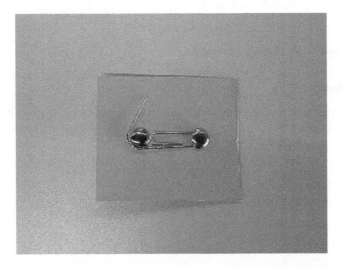

- Ask the children to create a simple circuit using crocodile clips, bulbs, bulb holders, battery packs and their switches. Test their circuits, with their switches, to make the bulbs go on and off. Model possible circuits to remind the children how a circuit works (this topic could link with work being covered in science).

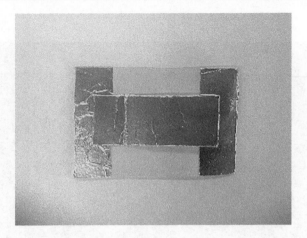

Now challenge children to design and make a light source with a switch and a hidden circuit. Discuss ideas, draw annotated sketches, cross-sectional drawings and exploded diagrams to generate the design criteria. CAD could be used for this.

- In pairs, small groups or individually, begin to construct the light source.

- Some children may require further support, so include templates that could be used.

- Encourage problem solving throughout the construction of their products.

- Test the completed products. Create a dark space and test how well their light sources illuminate.

(Continued)

(Continued)

Review and reflect

Discuss whether the completed light source meets the needs of the user and achieves its purpose.

Create an advert for the completed light source using iMovie. Share on the class blog for parents, carers and others in school to watch and comment on.

Assessment

- Children could sell their product back to the rest of the class, *Dragons' Den*-style. Discuss what makes their design special? Why do the materials they have used work well? What features do their light sources include?

- Use two stars and a wish for peer evaluation.

- Watch the completed adverts on iMovie. Would you buy their product? Discuss.

Follow-up activities

Ask the children to programme their torch automatically using a standalone box or an interface box to replace the switches and battery.

Test the design of different commercial switches, for example, a push-to-break switch (turned off by pressing) or a push-to-make switch (turned on by pressing), a toggle switch (when a lever is pressed) and a reed switch (using a magnet).

--- **ACTIVITY** ---

You Are What You Eat!

What you need to know

Working with food at Key Stage 1 and 2 is all about enabling children to understand where food comes from and the importance of eating a varied diet to keep healthy. The government has major concerns about the diet of children as eating habits are formed in childhood. As teachers we need to teach children the importance of a healthy balanced diet. The Eatwell Guide has been produced to give an idea of the percentages of the types of food we should eat.

The Eatwell Guide

See www.gov.uk/government/publications/the-eatwell-guide/the-eatwell-guide-how-to-use-in-promotional-material

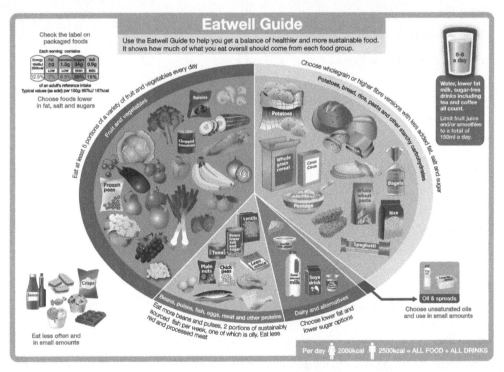

Source: https://assets.publishing.service.gov.uk/government/uploads/system/uploads/attachment_data/file/528193/Eatwell_guide_colour.pdf

The Eatwell Guide divides food into groups:

• Fruit and vegetables
• Bread, rice, potatoes and pasta

(Continued)

(Continued)

- Milk and dairy foods
- Meat, fish, eggs and beans
- Oils and spreads

Foods and drinks high in fat and/or sugar are to the side of the circle.

The size of the section on the plate relates to the amount we should have in our diet.

Design a healthy meal

Preparation

Discuss with children the types of foods they eat and what is good for them.

Objectives

To understand the importance of healthy eating.

To learn practical skills in food.

To work safely.

Curriculum links

D&T: design, make and evaluate; food and nutrition.

Science: healthy eating.

Mathematics: addition, percentages, measures.

Year groups

Years 4, 5 and 6, older children could use percentages.

Equipment

Basic kitchen equipment, various knives.

Useful links

Wider government healthy eating messages can be found on the NHS Choices website: www.nhs.uk

Food safety information and activities: www.food.gov.uk/sites/default/files/multimedia/pdfs/kitchen-check-yppack.pdf

Information: www.foodforum.org.uk

Free colouring posters: www.slippinsliders.com/food-coloring-pages-print

Online bread activities: www.grainchain.com/teachers/games

Setting the scene

Invite children to bring a container for their favourite drink. How much sugar is in your drink?

1. Look at the sugar content in different drinks.
2. The idea is to get children to recognise how much sugar is contained in drinks that they often consume.
3. Discussion can focus on ways of reducing the amount of sugar consumed in drinks and whether they are surprised by this.

Trigger questions

*   What foods are in the larger sections of the Eatwell Guide?
*   What are in the smaller sections; why should we eat less of these?
*   How can we reduce sugar in our diet?
*   What foods are considered 'salad' ingredients?
*   How should we prepare salad safely?
*   What are the rules when preparing food?

Time to experiment

Focused activities may include how to chop vegetables. Some vegetables, cabbage leaves or lettuce leaves can be torn or a butter knife can be used for softer fruit and vegetables. When using a sharp knife then the bridge and claw method should be used.

Video link on peeling, chopping and grating: www.foodafactoflife.org.uk

Design, Make and Evaluate challenge: children work in groups to design a healthy salad that could be included on the school lunch menu.

This is an iterative process, charting the relationship between children's ideas and how they are communicated and clarified through an activity.

Thought	Activity
What kind of salad are we going to make? Who will it be for? What shall we put in the salad? How will it look?	Discussion, drawing, written list, coming up with ideas.
How will I process the ingredients? What tools will I use? What skills do I need to use?	Discussion of what effect we want. Find out how to use the tools.
How can the processes we use create different effects?	Discussing and comparing. Trying out and evaluating.

(Continued)

(Continued)

Thought	Activity
What order are we going to work in? Who will do what?	Discussing, trying out, modifying the design.
How will we present the salad? Is our salad suitable for inclusion for the lunch menu at school?	Evaluating the product against our design criteria.

Children should make their salads taking care to work safe and clean.

Review and reflect

Children can taste one another's salads and decide which ones they like.

- How do we know our salad is healthy?
- Check the ingredients against the Eatwell Guide. In which groups are the ingredients?
- Are there any changes you could make? If so, what might you add or take away?

Assessment

Children make a 3-minute presentation about why their salad should be included on the school menu. They choose a name for their salad and talk about why they have selected particular ingredients.

Children listen to the presentations and decide whether they would include the salad in the school meals' menu. It would be a good idea to come up with some criteria for choosing the salad.

Follow-up activities

Children could apply their knowledge to discuss and decide on the school menu for a day or a week.

WEBSITES

Design and Technology Association website: www.data.org.uk

Education for Engineering website: https://educationforengineering.org.uk

Public Health England Eatwell Guide: www.gov.uk/government/publications/the-eatwell-guide

STEM learning website: www.stem.org.uk/resources/collection/2891/nuffield-primary-design-and-technology

6

FOREIGN LANGUAGES AND STEM

PAULINE PALMER AND SARAH LISTER

Science, technology, engineering and mathematics are all concerned with humans finding out about the world about them. Although first-hand experience is a vital part of exploring their world, learners gain much through sharing observations and insights with others. Being able to express one's ideas clearly, both to oneself and others, is a fundamental stepping-stone in developing a deeper understanding of a concept. Communicating one's ideas with precision is a vital skill, particularly when the subject matter at hand concerns how things are, how they came to be, how things work in our world and how we might improve them. Solving problems is also an essential element in all STEM related work, given that the disciplines originated from human attempts to be creative and to solve the problems encountered in everyday experiences.

IN THIS CHAPTER

The activities in this chapter are a useful starting point for using modern languages in STEM. Each project is practical in nature, designed to introduce and reinforce some key subject specific language and to address appropriate concepts in the teaching of science, technology and mathematics. As learners communicate and share their ideas and insights with increasing precision, their own understanding can deepen. Positive attitudes to the STEM subjects can be promoted within these different contexts.

Problem solving and investigation require the use of language, sometimes of a very specific nature. Using a second language requires learners to communicate very clearly, solving the problem of how to do this with sufficient precision that others can understand them. It also requires they make connections with what they already know. The processes of developing understanding through communication and communicating to explain what one understands go hand in hand. Giving learners the opportunity to work on language development alongside their growing understanding of the key ideas and concepts within the STEM subjects can enhance their aptitude and ability to make connections. All teachers, whatever their subject area, are fundamentally teachers of language, too (Kingman, 1988). Providing opportunities for the thoughtful and timely introduction of second language vocabulary can assist all learners in developing their ability to focus on key aspects of what they are doing, removing some of the 'background noise' that can detract from understanding. In addition, cross-curricular teaching can enable learners to make meaningful connections between different areas of the curriculum.

Our projects are designed to enable learners to make connections within the STEM subjects and to incorporate modern foreign languages into the curriculum in a meaningful, engaging and enjoyable way. They use French as the language medium, although other languages could be substituted, and enable the exploration of some key ideas and concepts related to science, mathematics, and design and technology, as well as literature and geography. For busy teachers, this can mean that the teaching of different subject areas can be combined and integrated. Using one of the STEM subjects as a context for language learning also offers a framework for those class teachers, who may lack confidence in another language, to locate their teaching of languages in areas of the curriculum with which they are more familiar.

The teaching of a modern foreign language is compulsory in England for children in Key Stage 2. Using a foreign language to explore the content and concepts from various areas of the curriculum is known as CLIL: Content and Language Integrated Learning. CLIL emerged in response to the demands and expectations of the modern age with globalisation, internationalisation and increasingly multilingual societies. Four elements are central to the CLIL approach: content, cognition, communication and culture (Coyle, 1999). Many countries in Europe already use this approach to help learn subject content using English as the teaching medium. Research indicates that learners make good progress in both content and language. Placing the emphasis on content rather than language has the potential to be mutually beneficial for both the content subject and the language. Marsh (2002) argues that the dual purpose and focus of CLIL pedagogy provides a more cognitively challenging and authentic platform for language acquisition and use, while providing meaningful and new contexts for learners to revisit key mathematical or scientific concepts.

Engaging with content through another language has been shown to lead to improvement in the development of children's problem solving and thinking skills. Exponents of CLIL extol the potential cognitive benefits of bilingualism (Baetens-Beardmore, 2008; Coyle et al., 2010) as well as the opportunities to promote creative thinking (Meehisto, 2008; Baker, 2011) through CLIL, what Marsh (2002) refers to as broadening 'thinking horizons'. Locating the teaching of STEM subjects in French can enable both teachers and learners to encounter new learning opportunities, to re-examine key concepts from a different perspective while maintaining cognitive demand.

Given the globalisation of society and the needs of employees in the future, linguistic competence is important. At primary school, learning another language can enhance children's awareness of the wider world, enabling them to make sense of who they are and can also develop a more inclusive classroom. For example, looking at sustainability in science, learners may explore a range of different perspectives on key elements. This can foster intercultural understanding, helping children to function as more informed global citizens in the future. Our projects can enable learners to locate various places on the globe and to explore some of the features of living in these countries, e.g. food, travel, culture. Using a modern foreign language as the teaching medium can enable learners to engage with key ideas and concepts in a different context, so that learners who may lack confidence in an area of the curriculum can visit the subject matter in a different way. It can offer opportunities for repetition in a different context and offers a real purpose for the use of the second language. Moreover, the use of a different language requires that learners develop precision in their use of language as they articulate key ideas, using appropriate vocabulary.

We have chosen three very different projects to demonstrate how the CLIL pedagogy can be utilised. Food related topics generally motivate children and any such activity is rich with possibilities for finding out about the role of foods in other cultures and making cross-curricular links. 'Pancakes' offers opportunities to focus on mathematical measurement, the properties of materials and how these change, and to explore cooking and nutrition in design and technology. 'Making Patterns' offers opportunities for learners to explore other cultures, to be creative and to investigate in a systematic way – essential elements in each of the STEM subjects. 'Planning a Journey' allows for exploration and problem solving with a purpose as well as enabling the children to draw upon their own experience. Along with the suggested projects, we also provide some of the key vocabulary and language structures that teachers and learners may need to engage fully. Bonne chance!

ACTIVITY

Make a patchwork patterned quilt

What you need to know

An exploration of patterns is an integral part of all mathematics as well as the foundation of algebra. Patterns are also a feature of natural objects and manmade structures.

Recognising, discussing, continuing or developing patterns provides an opportunity for learners to discuss characteristics, using descriptive vocabulary.

Creating patterns, using various media, such as paint, collage or textiles can enhance children's own understanding.

Preparation

Objectives

To make a patchwork pattern and develop the associated French vocabulary.

Curriculum links

Mathematics: reasoning – conjecturing relationships and developing an argument or justification, generate and describe number sequences.

Design and technology: design innovative, functional and appealing products, select and use tools and materials.

Art and design: use art and design techniques.

(Continued)

(Continued)

Modern languages: understand and respond to spoken language, speak with increasing confidence, fluency and spontaneity, engage in conversations.

RE: use of pattern in religious artefacts.

Year groups

Suitable for Years 3, 4, 5 and 6.

Equipment

Useful books: dependent on the year groups involved, pattern is a feature in books such as *Elmer the Elephant* and *The Patchwork Quilt*.

Sudoku games (see below).

Various coloured papers (or fabrics), rulers, glue and scissors, needles and thread.

Useful links

A useful source of patchwork images is www.nsaaquilting.co.uk/contact.php

Setting the scene

Teachers may choose to use either one of the suggested texts or an image to begin the discussion about patchwork patterns. For example, they could ask children if any of them had seen a bed quilt like the ones below:

French could be used when talking about the patterns and colours.

A simple Sudoku game could also be shown, explaining that a number or symbol can only appear once in each column and row.

(Continued)

(Continued)

Trigger questions

Regardez cette image	Look at this picture
Décrivez cette image	Describe this picture
Est-ce que vous pouvez predire ce qui suit?	Can you predict what comes next?
Comment vous le savez?	How do you know?
Faites un motif	Make a pattern
Quels materiaux utilisez-vous pour faire/créer votre motif?	What materials will you use to make your pattern?

Time to experiment

Children begin their own work by exploring a patterned quilt - preferably real, though images could be used. They could discuss the features (using the target language of colours, shapes etc., if possible) and be asked to record the sequence in some symbolic way, perhaps using squared paper.

They could practise giving instructions for what comes next to try to recreate this pattern, using the sequence of symbols they created.

They could also research quilts and quilting on the internet. Quilting has become an increasingly popular leisure pursuit over recent years and it may be possible for someone from a local group to come in to talk to the children, bringing examples of their work and explaining how they go about constructing them.

Using the materials provided (which could include various types of paper, glue and scissors or fabric, scissors, needles and thread) and scaffolding as appropriate, children then create their individual or small group patterns.

A nice pattern can be produced using a completed Sudoku as a starting point.

For example, in a Sudoku using the numbers one to four, all the fours could be covered with squares made up of one type and colour of paper, threes with a different one, etc. This can be used as a focus for discussion about area and perimeter, fractions or percentages.

4			
		3	
	1		
			2

Review and reflect

Children work to create their own patterns and talk about them, and the choices that they have made, as they work.

Assessment

The final product will provide evidence of the child's understanding and ideas.

Can another child explain the pattern sequence that has been used and predict what would come next? Can a child explain how they built up their pattern picture?

Follow-up activities

A class patchwork picture or quilt could be produced by joining together a 'pane' from each child, each pane incorporating a child's own pattern design.

(Continued)

(Continued)

Work on patchwork could also lead to an exploration of tessellation and to an investigation of which shapes tessellate and how these might be used or combined in a quilt.

Patchwork quilts were used by American slaves to communicate ideas – see www.covnews.com/archives/17383. Investigate the use of symbols to communicate, such as the formal mathematical symbols.

Children could look at how pattern is used in a particular context, for example in Islamic art.

Making patterns glossary

Les couleurs

bleu	blue
orange	orange
gris	grey
vert	green
rose	pink
violet	purple
rouge	red
noir	black
marron/brun	brown
blanc	white
jaune	yellow

Les formes

un triangle	a triangle
un rectangle	a rectangle
un cercle	a circle
un carré	a square
un hexagone	a hexagon
un pentagone	a pentagon
un octagone	an octagon
une ovale	an oval
un losange	a rhombus
un cerf Volant	a kite
un parallélogramme	a parallelogram

un trapeze	a trapezium
un triangle isocele	an isosceles triangle
un triangle équilatéral	an equilateral triangle
un triangle a un angle droit/avec un angle droit	a right angled triangle
un triangle avec un angle obtus	an obtuse angle triangle

Les chiffres

un	one
deux	two
trois	three
quatre	four
cinq	five
six	six
sept	seven
huit	eight
neuf	nine
dix	ten

Positional vocabulary

à gauche	to the left
à droit	to the right
au-dessous de	below
au-dessus de	above
au fond de	at the bottom/end of
au milieu de	in the middle of
au bord de	at the edge/side of
au bout de	after

Trigger questions

Regardez cette image	look at this image
Utilisez les peintres	use paints
Decris ce motif/dessin	tell me about/describe this pattern
Le motif/dessin est ...	the pattern is ...

(Continued)

(Continued)

Est-ce que tu peux predire ce qui suit?	Can you predict what follows?
Je peux predire que c'est …	I can predict that it's …
Comment tu le sais?	How do you know?
Je sais parce qu'il y a …	I know because there are …
Fais un motif/dessin	make a pattern
Qu'est-ce que tu vas utiliser?	What are you going to use?
Je vais utiliser …	I am going to use …
les peintres	paints
le papier de couleur	coloured paper
le tissu	fabric
les règles	rulers
la colle	glue
les cisseaux	scissors
une aiguille	a needle
un fil	a thread

ACTIVITY

Make a Crepe for Pancake Day

What you need to know

Some form of pancakes or omelets are a popular food in many cultures, e.g. tortilla in Spain, blinis in Scandinavia and crepes in France. Different fillings and presentations could be explored as part of this activity.

Sometimes, these food stuffs are linked to special celebrations and religious festivals. Pancake day relates to using up food resources prior to the fasting associated with Lent.

Many, including pancakes and crepes, use eggs, flour and milk as a basis. When these are combined within the mixtures, there are changes and there are further changes of state when the mixture is cooked.

Pupils will need to know the basic rules of food hygiene, and attention will need to be paid to your school's health and safety policy.

Preparation

Objectives

To make a crepe and develop the associated French vocabulary.

Curriculum links

Mathematics: measurement and scaling, convert between different units of metric measure, ratio and proportion.

Science: properties of materials, states of matter.

Design and technology: understand and apply the principles of nutrition and learn how to cook.

Modern languages: understand and respond to spoken language; speak with increasing confidence, fluency and spontaneity; engage in conversations.

RE: history of religious festivals and particular foods.

Year groups

Years 3 and 4, work on ratio and proportion could extend this to Years 5 and 6.

(Continued)

(Continued)

Equipment

Foodstuffs – eggs, milk and flour, toppings for the pancakes, such as fruit; equipment – scales, measuring jugs, spoons, bowls, whisks plus the use of a stove and plates and forks to serve and implements required for preparing toppings such as knives and chopping boards.

Setting the scene

This may be part of a wider topic, for example looking at festivals or special events in one's own life or culture and that of others. Some work could relate to personal anecdotes and memories initially, before using secondary sources of evidence. News items, pictorial images or videos could be used as a stimulus and to support the work.

Depending on the time of year, this activity could be linked to pancake day, or to stories, or it could be part of an exploration of changes of state or the senses in science.

Teachers may then go on to talk about what is planned, the production of the crepes and explain what a crepe is (some children may already know about them and can explain).

Reminders about health and safety and food hygiene need to be given in English.

The teacher then explains that the lesson will now proceed in French.

Trigger questions

Teachers can ask basic questions to introduce the relevant vocabulary, for example, holding up an egg and asking 'Qu'est-ce que c'est?' (visual prompt cards could be used).

Teachers could also ask is this liquid or solid? What are you going to do/what do we need to do next (actions).

The teacher then demonstrates what to do, explaining in French, as the various elements are carried out. At each point, ask the children to repeat the phrase:

English	French
Measure the flour	Mesurez la farine
Beat the eggs	Battez les oeufs
Add the eggs to the flour	Ajoutez les oeufs à la farine
Mix in the milk to make a batter	Melangez le lait pour faire un pate

Given that the crepes are then fried, teachers may prefer to do this step for themselves as a demonstration. Once this has been demonstrated for one group, others may use some of the time to clear up their group workspaces or to prepare fillings, for example, slicing lemons, melting chocolate or grating cheese.

Time to experiment

The children work in small groups. At each step, after watching the teacher, the children then give instructions as to what to do. Teachers may wish to allocate specific roles for each child in the group, for example, one to give the instructions, one to measure, one to mix and one to report back.

Review and reflect

The teacher checks, at each point, whether the children have completed the step, before moving on. They could ask questions such as, 'what does the mixture look like now?'

- Children could engage in some statistical work related to their favourite fillings.
- Children could consider how to scale the quantities up or down for given numbers of people, exploring ratio and proportion.

Assessment

Children could assess each other's contributions to the final product, considering for example, how good they were at following instructions.

This activity could also be used to assess children's ability to sequence the steps and use the associated vocabulary.

(Continued)

(Continued)

Follow-up activities

- Children could work in small groups to engage in research, exploring similarities and differences between pancakes and crepes and other similar foodstuffs, discussing which country these might originate from.

- Each group could make one or more of the dishes they have researched for others to try. The class could then vote for their favourite dish.

- The class could produce a recipe book for parents and carers.

- They may also discuss the significance of Pancake Day in the Christian year, as preceding Lent and go on to discuss other special foods associated with religious and cultural festivals.

- They could use the information gained to make posters, information leaflets or as a stimulus for creative writing.

Making a pancake glossary

Qu'est-ce que c'est?	What is it?
C'est ...	It is ...
Est-ce que c'est solide ou liquide?	Is it solid or liquid?
Qu'est-ce qu'il faut faire?	What do we need to do?

Il faut ...	We need/have to ...
Mesurez la farine	measure the flour
Mesurez cent dix grammes de farine	measure 110 grams of flour
Ajoutez deux cent millilitres de lait	add 200 ml of milk
Battez les oeufs	beat the eggs
Ajoutez les oeufs à la farine	add the eggs to the flour
Mélangez le lait	stir/mix the milk
Faites une pate	make a batter
Utlisez cinquante grammes de beurre pour frire la crepe	Use 50 grams of butter to fry the crepe
Utilisez la poele pour faire frire la crepe	Use the frying pan to fry your pancake
Qu'est ce que tu vas ajouter à ta crepe?	What will you add to your pancake?
Je vais ajouter ...	I am going to add ...
le sucre	sugar
le citron	lemon
le chocolat	chocolate
le fromage	cheese
j'aime ... le mieux ...	I like ... the best
Ma garniture preféree, c'est ...	My favourite topping is ...

Ratio and proportion

For example:

Il faut ajouter combien des oeufs/de farine/du lait pour quatre personnes?

How much/many eggs/flour/milk do you need to add for four people?

ACTIVITY

Planning a Journey

What you need to know?

This activity offers a meaningful context for mathematics and allows for problem solving and enquiry. It provides a context for the use of a range of modern languages vocabulary that may be required in real life. Planning and going on journeys to other countries may

(Continued)

(Continued)

require reading information, speaking and listening in the language of the host country. Focusing on a specific destination also enables children to develop their understanding of other countries. This project could include some computer use, such as researching relevant information and use of a spreadsheet to determine costs. It could also lead to discussion and to comparison of the environmental impact of various modes of transport, such as the carbon footprint of travelling by train as opposed to by aeroplane. It may also be part of a wider unit on transport or motion.

Preparation

Objectives

To plan a journey and develop the associated French vocabulary.

Curriculum links

Mathematics: reasoning, problem solving with measures.

Modern languages: understand and respond to spoken language, speak with increasing confidence, fluency and spontaneity, engage in conversations.

Geography: locational knowledge.

Year groups

Years 5 and 6.

Equipment

A globe, a map of Europe with an integral scale, a trundle wheel, metre sticks. This mathematically based practical activity could be accompanied by internet research to determine data such as fuel consumption for a chosen car, cost of fuel and the likely time required to make the journey.

For the extension activities: data from airlines, train and ferry companies (including both costs and timings for each), bus and taxi services (the children could research this information for themselves).

Useful links

Materials produced by the Shell Centre: www.mathshell.com/materials.php?series=numeracy&item =planatrip

It may be helpful to have some small model people to illustrate a variety of travellers for the follow-up activities.

Setting the scene

(Continued)

(Continued)

Encourage children to consider the journeys that they make, beginning with their own journey to school each day. They could make a simple map and explain their route to a partner (using some of the target positional activity from the 'Making Patterns' project). They could then be asked to think of some of the longer journeys they have made, perhaps going on holiday. They could discuss distances, time taken and modes of travel. They could be asked to think of journeys that others might take. This could link with contemporary items in the media, or to factual work on adult occupations and roles, or to stories in which a character chooses to go on a journey.

Teachers may wish to create their own scenario for why a character might want to go on a specific journey to a named destination.

Mark two points on the classroom floor, labelled 'Outset' and 'Destination' to represent the journey. The distance between the points should be proportional to the true distance. Children measure the distance using a trundle wheel or tape measure. Depending on the class, provide the scale so children can calculate the actual distance. Children can research the journey distance on maps or the internet and possible costs of different modes of transport.

Trigger questions (in French)

Comment est-ce qu'on peut voyager pour arriver à …?	How might we travel to get there?
Il faut combien de temps pour arriver, par exemple en voiture?	How long would it take us to get there, for example, travelling by car?
Ca coute combien?	How much would it cost?
Est-ce que vous puvez calculer la distance de … à …?	Can you calculate the distance from … to …?

Time to experiment

While some groups undertake research, others work in small groups to decide how they are going to work out the distance indicated by the outset and destination labels on the classroom floor, using the equipment provided to physically measure the distance. Where possible, all counting of units and instructions should be in the target language. Once all children have had the opportunity to do both the research and the measurement, they can compare information and assess the accuracy of their methods.

Teachers may allocate specific roles for children, such as manager, scribe, or technical support (taking the actual measurement and/or completing the calculations).

Having established the distance, children are then able to work out how much it might cost to travel by car, using information either provided by the teacher or from their own research, on fuel consumption. They can also estimate how long the journey might take and how much it might cost.

Review and reflect

- Did all the groups find similar information?
- How accurate was the classroom measurement?
- Which mode of transport is likely to be most cost effective?
- What other things might need to be considered?

Assessment

Children can assess how they worked together as a group, how they managed the requisite activities and the accuracy of their answers.

Children present their findings to the other groups in French.

Follow-up activities

Having decided on their own preferred mode of travel, children could explore how a series of different characters might choose to travel, for example, a business person, a family with children, two students on a gap year … explaining why each set of characters may wish to travel in different ways, looking at costs, time taken and other factors.

They could also look at the Nuffield Trust materials, such as 'How far can you travel in an hour': www.nuffieldfoundation.org/applying-mathematical-processes/every-second-counts

Planning a journey glossary

Nous voyageons à …	We are travelling to …
Est-ce que tu peux trouver … sur une carte/un globe?	Can you find … on a map/globe?
Comment est-ce qu'on peut calculer la distance?	How can you calculate the distance?
de (outset location) à …?	from (outset location) to …?
Voici (location)	Here is (location)
Est-ce que tu peux calculer cette distance?	Can you calculate this distance?
C'est … centimetres/metres	It is … centimetres/metres
Voici une eschelle	Here is a scale
Est-ce que tu peux utiliser cette eschelle pour transformer?	Can you use this scale to convert?
Comment est-ce qu'on peut voyager pour arriver à …?	How might you travel to get to …?
Je peux voyager en bateau/en avion/en voiture/en train	I can travel by boat/by plane/by car/by train

(Continued)

(Continued)

Il faut combien de temps pour arriver?	How long would it take to get there?
Il faut/prend une heure/deux heures/une journée	It will take an hour/two hours /a day
Il faut calculer le prix de ...	You need to calculate the cost of ...
l'essence	petrol
la nourriture/les repas	food/meals
la traversée du ferry	ferry crossing

Using a modern foreign language as the medium for learning and teaching STEM helps children develop their communication skills and scientific thinking. In the primary classroom, regular use of a modern foreign language will help to develop children's familiarity and confidence with the vocabulary and everyday phraseology. The CLIL approach helps children to appreciate the relevance and power of the modern foreign language.

REFERENCES

Baetens-Beardsmore, H. (2008) Multilingualism, cognition and creativity. *International CLIL Research Journal*, 1(1), 4-19.

Baker, C. (2011) *Foundations of Bilingual Education and Bilingualism*. Bristol: Multilingual Matters.

Coyle, D. (1999) Theory and planning for effective classrooms: supporting students in content and language integrated learning contexts. In J. Masih (ed.), *Learning Through a Foreign Language*. London: CILT.

Coyle, D., Hood, P. & Marsh, D. (2010) *CLIL: Content and Language Integrated Learning*. Cambridge: Cambridge University Press.

Kingman. (1988) *Report of the Committee of Inquiry into the Teaching of English Language*. London: HMSO.

Marsh, D. (2002) *Using Languages to Learn and Learning to Use Languages*. Milan: TIE-CLIL.

Meehisto, P. (2008) CLIL counterweights: recognizing and decreasing disjuncture in CLIL. *International CLIL Journal*, 1(1), 93-112.

7
DRAMA AND STEM

REBECCA PATTERSON, MICK CHESTERMAN AND ALISON RAMSAY

Drama is about exploring human nature. In order to navigate and learn about the world in which we live, we have to understand contexts as well as concepts. We tend to place ourselves and our own prior experience at the centre of the learning process and then begin to make connections between what we think we know and new ideas we encounter. Learning is not a linear, cumulative process and drama understands and accommodates this. Drama, like STEM, involves a process of discovery and when curiosity is ignited, participants are encouraged to work and learn together by drawing upon the prior experience and knowledge of all the participants rather than relying on the notion of teacher as the 'one who knows'. In such contexts, teachers are able to facilitate learners in a process of finding meaning and purpose in what they are doing.

IN THIS CHAPTER

In this chapter, we offer two activities, which demonstrate the potential for collaboration between drama and STEM in primary teaching and learning contexts. There is a correspondence between the process of dramatic inquiry (i.e. problem solving through the enactment of events) and the problem-solving processes in mathematics and science. By utilising the idea of project based learning but with a further layer of learning experience emerging from the creation of fictional contexts, activities are driven largely by the learners' decision making. The same suggests there may not be definitive outcomes but the learning experience will be rich and long lasting.

At the end of this chapter there is a glossary of terms pertaining to drama techniques and conventions (denoted by * in the text) that may not be familiar.

Drama relies on fictional contexts; that does not mean that the real world no longer exists but rather, learning takes place by negotiating understandings between both realms. In the make believe situation anything is possible. For example, imagine beginning a lesson with this opening narrative:

> The commander had told us to count to ten and then to pull hard on the ripcord. Suddenly, after feeling like my teeth were being pushed to the back of my head, I was experiencing the most wonderful, exhilarating feeling. As we looked down, the land below us was growing closer but somehow it didn't look right. Instead of the fields and rivers that our maps told us would be there, we were descending over a small town and we seemed to be heading towards a school playground.
>
> Finally, we landed, knees bent, feet first just as we had been taught. Then as most of us lost our balance, as gravity took over, we rolled over onto the tarmac, and apart from the swoosh of nylon parachute all around us, there was silence. The jump had taken just minutes, the experience would last forever.

If you then ask your learners, 'If this were you, who do you think you might be and why are you here?', you would be drawing the learners further into the fiction and grabbing their attention as well as their imagination. By using their response and ideas to develop your planning, it is possible to address STEM topics such as gravity, speed, time etc., but at the same time, acknowledging the learners' input that can lead to increased levels of engagement.

The process of learning does not occur in bite sized chunks called 'knowledge'. It is a constant embodied as much as a cerebral process and, therefore, it is important to help learners to access the curriculum in as many ways as possible. Using story-telling as an approach to teaching and learning, as drama does, enables us to tap into the learners' innate inventiveness, creativity, curiosity and imagination. By doing so, we are able to suspend reality and to visit other worlds. It is in such spaces that we sometimes find it easier to articulate our ideas and to accept there are experiences that lie beyond our own; in other words, we learn to empathise with others.

ACTIVITY

Finding Life 'Out There'

What you need to know

Before the project begins you need to gather all necessary resources as listed below. When using drama for the first time it is a good idea to create a contract that relates to issues of behaviour. For example, you may need to explain that the whole class, including you, the teacher, is going to begin the project by working in role. It is important children listen carefully and they respond to you in role-play as appropriate. If this is the first time you have used this technique with this class, it may be a good idea to offer a quick demonstration. Learners will be expected to work in groups, be prepared to share their ideas and to accept the ideas of others.

This dramatic inquiry uses the pre-text[*] of a group of newly qualified astronauts who are being sent on a mission to search for life beyond the solar system. It follows the 2016 discovery of an apparently rocky planet orbiting the nearest star to our sun, which is thought to be at least 1.3 times the mass of the Earth. The planet lies within the so-called habitable zone of the star Proxima Centauri, or Proxima b as it has become known, meaning that liquid water could potentially exist on this newly discovered world. The discovery of this rocky planet in the habitable zone around our sun's nearest star will mark the beginning of decades of intense research and exploration.

Preparation

Objectives

- To investigate how stars are formed.
- To consider the possibility of other forms of life in the universe.
- To develop group work skills.

Curriculum links

Mathematics: measures including time and distance.

Science: the solar system, the universe, life forms, effects of space travel on humans.

Design and technology: planning the layout of a space ship (optional).

Philosophy: asking and exploring questions for which there are no simple answers.

English: reflective writing about feelings.

Drama: developing skills to work co-operatively and adopt a role.

Year groups

Years 4, 5 and 6.

Equipment

Large space. Astronaut certificates. Name badge for Chief Training Officer of AAE (Academy of Astronomical Excellence). Costume signifier for Astronauts. Music.

Useful links

www.theguardian.com/science/2016/aug/24/earth-like-planet-found-orbiting-our-suns-nearest-star-raises-hopes-for-life-proxima-b

www.stem.org.uk/elibrary/list/16611/space-7-9-year-olds

www.makewav.es/story/961130/title/diaryentryiamtimpeake

https://mantleoftheexpert.com

Setting the scene

Beginning with Teacher in Role (TIR)[*] as the Chief Training Officer in the AAE leading the briefing in 2066 in preparation for the newly qualified astronauts' first mission:

(Continued)

(Continued)

Good afternoon all, class of 2066. I am delighted to be here with you all today. Your final graduation day is over and you are about to embark upon your first mission. As I look around me now and see you all, older and wiser and ready to explore the universe, I see the best trained astronauts in the world and we are all very proud of you. As your tutor I am particularly proud of you. There are a couple of quick training exercises that we must complete before you receive your final certificate in order to ensure you are fully fit and able to control the ship cooperatively. You may be out there for a long time and it is important that you are able to work as a team. Once this is done, you will begin the preparations for your first mission which I must emphasise, is TOP SECRET and EYES-ONLY. All that remains to be said is good luck!

Trigger questions

- Why do you think the mission might be top secret?
- Why do scientists explore space?
- What is it like to be an astronaut?

Time to experiment

Warm up exercise

This can be framed as being a typical training exercise for astronauts. The game is called 'Star Catchers'. Ask pupils to find their own space in the room/hall. Tell them that they are all lights floating in the night sky. Choose one pupil to be the Star Catcher. The Star Catcher stands in the centre of the room and all the lights (the rest of the class) must move around them (you can use music to add atmosphere).

The leader (usually the teacher) says 'Lights to star bright . . . 1, 2, 3, 4, 5'. All the 'lights' get into groups of 5. They now form a five pointed star by putting their left hands together in the centre of a circle and stretching their right arms out like the rays of a star. Count again to 5. On the number 5, the Star Catcher tries to catch any spare lights that are floating about by touching them on the shoulder. Any lights that are caught become Star Catchers and collect in one place until there are no more left floating. The stars break up and the game continues with leader/teacher picking another Star Catcher.

The Star Catchers work together to try and corner spare lights and the lights work together by trying to distract the Star Catchers. You can speed up or slow down the numbers counted to help the lights or the Star Catchers.

Move back into TIR as the Chief of AAE

Learners are given the following information as they remain in role as astronauts.

Well done troops. You worked really well as a team and this bodes well for your mission. As I said before, this mission is eyes-only, in other words, top-secret, so you must not discuss it with anyone outside the academy. The mission is of huge significance in the development of astrophysics and for our knowledge of the universe outside of our solar system.

You are to lead a mission to the planet known as Proxima b, which was first discovered in 2016 before any of us were born, even me! At the time it was discovered there was a flurry of excitement as it offered a tantalising possibility that it might be similar in crucial respects to Earth. Fifty years on, we are now pretty sure that there is an expectation that this planet may be hosting life forms. Your mission is to reach this new planet. Once you have landed safely, you will be given further instructions. We believe that it is safer for you all not to know any more at this stage in case there is a leak. If this happens, the mission will be aborted immediately. Are there any questions?

It may be at this stage learners will have questions they want to ask out of role, as well as in-role as astronauts. This is fine and you can formally leave the role-play to address these questions and have a discussion about what has just happened. As suggested in the introduction, the fictional context and the real world co-exist and any questions or moments of reflection are crucial to the learning process.

Back as TIR:

So, you will be leaving first thing tomorrow. I suggest you get a good night's sleep. Before then, as none of you will have the chance to speak to your loved ones, I would like you all to write a brief letter to a person of your choice.

This activity introduces the idea of writing in role and it enables learners to reflect on the learning that has taken place. If appropriate, this could be set as a homework activity. Remember to re-iterate the fact that the mission is 'eyes-only'.

Defining space*:

As class teacher, ask the learners how they think the space ship would be laid out inside. This could be done as a project in design and technology, but what we are aiming for is to create the inside of the space ship in the classroom or hall so that we can imagine being on the ship as it lands on Proxima b.

On the ship:

TIR leads the learners from the real world back into the fictional world.

Welcome on board the space ship. As you can see, it is very small and lacking in a few home comforts but this will be your home for the next six months.

To make you realise just how amazing this experience is and to give you an idea of how much we have moved on in the last 50 years I have been down in the academy archive and retrieved this diary entry from someone who took part in a space mission in 2015/16. It seems so old fashioned now but here it is.

(Continued)

(Continued)

Tuesday 15 December 2015

Dear Diary,

Here I was in the vast open world of an extraordinary site, Space. This was my dream to venture out into another world that is incredible to see, I will cherish the moment for life when in Kazakhstan I got into my space uniform and proudly entered the expensive space craft that was about to set off. At 11:03 I was waved off into space by my mum and dad who stood about 200m away from the launch site with tears of happiness pouring from their eyes. As a member of NASA I believe in myself and all of the people on board this space craft to find out more about exciting discoveries in space. For a training programme on-board this spacecraft I have to do at least two and a half hours of exercise every single day otherwise my body would react to the zero gravity out in space and we would start to lose some of the bone density in our body. When entering space I grew seven centimetres taller due to the zero gravity up in space that causes the body to elongate.

Of course, as you will be aware, we have developed the technology that can now counteract these gravitational effects so you don't need to worry about growing any taller! Never the less, you are probably all feeling similarly nervous about the trip. I wonder if you might want to share some of your letters home with us just so that we can better understand how you are all feeling at the moment.

Again you can come out of role to organise this next stage but that will depend on your group and on levels of confidence with reading.

Narrate the next section as the learners take their places on the ship.

Once the astronauts were safely on board, the computers were programmed and there was no turning back.

(If possible, change the lighting in the room and play some music.)

Their six month journey was beginning. All their training was now being put to the test. The feelings of weightlessness, as if being suspended in mid-air were disconcerting but not unexpected. It was also difficult to keep track of time. The ship's computer guided them out of the Earth's atmosphere and soon they were deep in space.

During this phase, you could use thought-tracking[*] to help establish how well the learners are engaging and what they are thinking in role.

Soon they began to orbit the new planet, Proxima b. Below the ship, the planet seemed to hover. It was beautiful. Blue oceans, dark green forests, magnificent mountains, it looked like paradise. On the second orbit each crew member began to get ready for disembarking. They made their way to the viewing gallery, and watched the beautiful sight beneath them as they dressed themselves in their space suits and protective helmets.

Creating the landscape and small group drama

Out of role, ask the learners to draw maps of the planet as they imagine it, or from research they may have done prior to the lesson. Share the ideas that have been generated and discuss what kinds of specialisms the astronauts might have in terms of studying the planet. This may have already been decided in the preliminary stages but if not, the class needs to be divided into small groups and each group should decide what specialist roles they want to play, e.g. archaeologists, food scientists, geologists. The next stage is going to involve structuring a piece of drama that shows the astronauts exploring the planet. This can be set up by giving the astronauts further instructions via satellite link (i.e. email, text message).

Instructions

> Congratulations on your safe and well executed landing. Now you have landed, we would like you to document what you find. You will do this by creating three photographic images per group and we would like you to write a title for each image you create so that we have a clear log of your activities. This information is vital to us on Earth and you will need to send it via satellite link as soon as possible.

Ask the groups to create a series of three still images* documenting their expedition on the planet's surface. Give them a short amount of time to plan (no more than 10 minutes). In addition to the still images, you are asking the learners to write a caption for each one as if they were photographic images with subtitles.

When you think they are ready, the groups can perform their still images simultaneously as a practice run before they send them to Earth via satellite link. Consider where the groups are in relation to each other and if possible, give each group a different corner of the room. Ask them to share their images again but this time they will do it one at a time and hold it as still as possible. As each group shares their sequence of three images you can use what you see and their captions to help underscore with narrative. For example, if one of their captions says something like 'searching for life' you could narrate:

> The biologists gently gather samples of plant life and water. They bag them up and place them carefully in the specially designed crates to take back for examination in the ship's laboratory. Meanwhile the archaeologists begin their search for fossils by digging into the cliff face.

This section is essentially orchestrated by you, but the content is driven by the learners' ideas, knowledge and imagination.

The dilemma

There are several ways this next section can be set up, but the idea is essentially that the astronauts will discover a living being very similar to themselves. As they are searching the planet they receive another message from Earth:

(Continued)

(Continued)

> These are your final instructions. We have reason to believe that there is life similar to that of human beings on Proxima b and therefore, it is your duty as citizens of Earth to capture and bring back any life forms you find. This is an order and it is why your mission must remain top secret.

- Option 1: TIR as the alien being who meets the astronauts. The group hot seat* the alien and discover that the species is at risk of extinction. She pleads with them not to take her to Earth. Out of role the group is asked to take a vote.

- Option 2: Learner in role (LIR)* as the alien following the same format as above.

- Option 3: The scenario is narrated. Similarly, a vote is taken. If the group lacks experience and confidence, this may be the best option but it tends not to create the same atmosphere and sense of a dilemma as building a connection between the astronauts and the alien does.

Once the vote has been made, the decision is final. Either the alien is left alone on the planet, meaning that their orders have not been carried out, or they vote to take her with them. In both cases there will be consequences, which they will have to face as the dilemma continues.

Review and reflect

See above, writing/reading in role.

Use open questions to explore learner response. For example:

- What have we explored in the drama today?

- Encourage further discussion to help with planning for a possible follow-up lesson by asking them what they would like to explore next.

Assessment

Formative assessment opportunities throughout the process using questions and answers, reflective writing and thought-tracking.

Follow-up activities

Create a news report about the expedition using digital technology/script writing/further research. Investigate the effects of space on the human body.

Investigate the distances involved and the likely times of travel between planets.

Investigate society's attitudes towards 'aliens'.

— ACTIVITY —

Digital Braves

Young people are growing up tracked. Digital technology means that by the time they reach adulthood, they already have a complex and compromised online footprint. This tracking is linked to our identities as consumers and the digital choices we make every day. It is also the case that data are held and increasingly traded by governments, global corporations and cyber criminals. So, what are our digital rights and why do we often give them away so freely?

This activity sets out to explore this issue through the imagined context of a near future new social order in which people are re-categorised as either Creatives or Consumers. It is rooted in what Rainer and Lewis (2012) identify as 'authentic learning' through drama, and seeks to motivate learners by locating encounters with technology within a fictitious world that feels 'real', challenging them to respond in complex ways to emerging themes and ideas. From within the dramatic frame, participants are encouraged to explore what it might mean to live in such a world, to experiment 'hands-on' with technology and software, and to examine the new pressures and implications of commercial digital surveillance through a combination of role play and Webmaking. Mozilla's Thimble, a tool that encourages exploratory learning by remixing HTML pages in the browser, is also used to demystify coding and digital production, enabling participants to interact playfully with digital material and content generated by the drama. This work is inspired by and adds to the recent Webmaking work done by Mozilla surrounding Digital and Web Literacies, enabling participants to make web objects using simple online tools.

By using technology in playful ways to provoke questions about the digitised world we all now inhabit, this drama seeks to move beyond discussions of the place and potential of new technologies in drama classrooms (Anderson, 2012; Rainer & Lewis, 2012). Instead, it is responsive to Michael Anderson's (2014) call to acknowledge drama education as a potentially powerful tool for navigating the complexity, chaos and contradictions of 'post-normal' contemporary existence, in which rapid technological innovation and all pervasive networked systems play a significant role.

The work has been trialled in a variety of contexts, including with children attending a home schooling group associated with Edlab at Manchester Metropolitan University. It was also delivered as part of London Mozfest 2017, an annual event focused on raising and debating issues of internet control and privacy, and The Digital Activism conference held in Manchester in 2016.

Part one: thinking about data and data-tracking

Making choices

Give each participant a copy of the following template. This can be adapted as necessary to suit the needs/interests of the participants taking part in the drama.

(Continued)

(Continued)

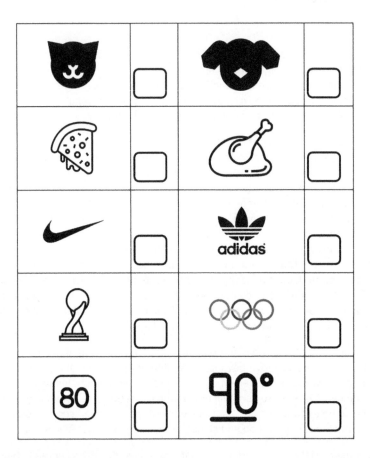

Now ask each participant to stand on their own in the space. When you call out the options provided, they must indicate their preference by moving to the left or right side of the room (i.e. cat lover – move to the left, dog lover – move to the right). Inform them that they must MAKE a decision, even if they like or dislike both options.

Introduce the Target story:

An angry man went into a Target store outside of Minneapolis, demanding to talk to a manager.

'My daughter got this in the mail!' he said. 'She's still in high school, and you're sending her coupons for baby clothes and cribs? Are you trying to encourage her to get pregnant?'

The manager didn't have any idea what the man was talking about. He looked at the mail. Sure enough, it was addressed to the man's daughter and contained advertisements for maternity clothing, nursery furniture and pictures of smiling infants. The manager apologised and then called a few days later to apologise again.

On the phone, though, the father was somewhat abashed. 'I had a talk with my daughter,' he said. 'It turns out her baby is due in August. I owe you an apology.'

Ask participants to discuss the following key questions in pairs or small groups:

- How do you think Target knew the man's daughter was pregnant?
- How does this story relate to what we have just done?

Use the responses as the basis for a discussion about how our shopping habits in the 'real' world and 'online' are tracked and used by retailers/companies to target us through online adverts. Target knew the daughter was pregnant because it had been tracking her shopping habits and purchases. The 'making choices' exercise might be said to mirror this process. Participants made explicit choices without knowing why they were asked to do so. In moving to an area of the room to make that choice, they created a visual trail that could be tracked. Finally, the template captured their choices, providing useful data on their personal preferences that can be used to 'target' them in the future.

Tell the group these data are going to be used as a starting point for our drama. Each choice is assigned a point (see below). Individuals add up their points to calculate their Consumer Value.

Example scores are listed below.

Dog	9	Cat	5
Pizza	3	Fried chicken	9
Nike	2	Adidas	5
World Cup	3	Olympics	8
1980s music	2	1990s music	8

Once scores have been calculated, ask the group to organise themselves in numerical order, high to low, diagonally across the room. They should occupy all the room by spreading out evenly in one line. Split the line and label those with the lowest score Group One, and those with the highest score Group Two.

Part two: entering the fictional world

Show a video that outlines the dramatic context (see resources page at http://goo.gl/W33zkO). Below is a transcript of the accompanying commentary that outlines the key ideas underpinning the drama to come.

With human labour no longer necessary due to the development of advanced robot technologies, people are re-categorised as either Creatives or Consumers. They attend

(Continued)

(Continued)

different schools, live in different parts of town, and perform very different roles. For the Creatives, work means the endless production of high quality adverts and messages designed to sell 'products' to targeted Consumers. While the Consumers earn their living by continually selecting and purchasing these products via social media and the internet, now controlled by a mysterious organisation known only as the Network.

As the film is shown, the teacher adopts the role of Spokesperson for the Network by putting on a simple item of costume. This character should adopt a firm but fair manner and project a positive outlook on the new social order that the film outlines. Taking influence from some of our own 'real' world politicians, the Spokesperson also seems to find a way of responding to questions without ever really providing answers.

Teacher-in-Role (TIR) as a Spokesperson for the Network:

Welcome Citizens. Our recent history has been challenging. The crisis that led to the Great Wars meant we had to find a new way of organising our economy and society. We now believe we have found that way. I know you are as excited as we are about the future. Therefore, we will waste no time in getting started.

TIR - To Group One:

Your data have determined that you will now occupy the role of Consumers. Your role will be to consume continually in order to keep our new economy going. You will receive a daily allowance of $200 to spend. If your choices are good, this will increase. However, bad choices will incur penalties and a reduction in your allowance.

TIR - To Group Two:

From your data, we have concluded that you will fulfil the role of Creatives. You will use your talents to produce the advertisements and messages from which the Consumers will make their choices. Your basic needs will be provided for but this provision will increase or decrease according to the quality of your creative output.

Soon you will say your farewells and begin your initial training. However, we have a little time to take any questions you may have regarding our new arrangements.

Ask each group to discuss and identify questions arising from the new social order that has been outlined. It might be useful to play the video again to help prompt these.

The meeting

As the Spokesperson for the Network, TIR calls the groups back together and takes questions. Use the device of TIR to 'play' with the questions in such a way as to provoke emotive and thoughtful responses in the participants. Equally, lines of enquiry can be extended or nudged in a particular direction.

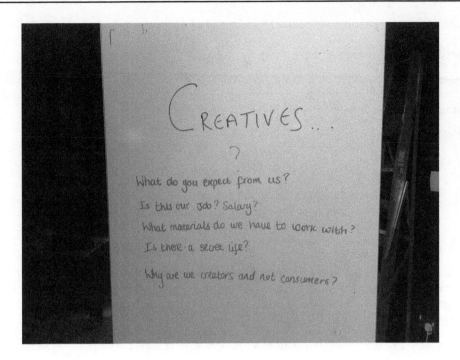

When you sense all questions have been asked and all avenues explored, bring the meeting and the drama to a close.

TIR as Spokesperson:

> Thank you Citizens. We hope things are now clearer in your mind. Please say your goodbyes and make your way to the transport waiting to take you to your new places of residence. Today marks the moment of our new beginning and together we will build a better future.

Allow participants to respond briefly to the above before instructing each group to file out of the meeting in an orderly fashion.

Out of role reflection

- How did you feel about the job role you were assigned?
- Would you be happy with the lifestyles on offer?
- Can we see parallels with our world today?

(Continued)

(Continued)

Part three: consuming and creating

TIR, as Network Spokesperson, calls the Creatives and Consumers back together. Each group sits on opposite sides of the room facing a whiteboard. In addition, groups will need to have access to laptops/terminals in order to carry out the web-making activities.

Training:

TIR – as Spokesperson:

> Greetings Citizens. We are talking to you all today via video link. Today Creatives will be receiving basic training in the creation and dissemination of advertising material. Consumers, you have been invited to watch this demonstration with a view to enabling you to make informed consumer choices.

Either TIR as Network Spokesperson or an additional character known as the Assistant (AIR) demonstrates how to create adverts using the coding tools. In the original sessions, this additional character enabled collaborative work within the world of the drama between drama and computing specialists.

AIR, as technical support, demonstrates how to create adverts using the Mozilla Thimble tool:

> As you may know, the Network is a series of simple memes or adverts designed to catch the Consumer's attention and sell them products. All targeted messages start with a very simple advert. We can see a basic phone advert here – https://goo.gl/CBdfKe

As you can see, it is very basic. The job of the Creatives is to alter the text of the advert and even the image used. To do this you must hit the REMIX button on the screen. You will see the page open in CREATIVE mode with the advert on the right and the code on the left. This is HTML code, which powers the Network. As an example, when you change the text on line 13 on the left, the advert is updated straight away on the right.

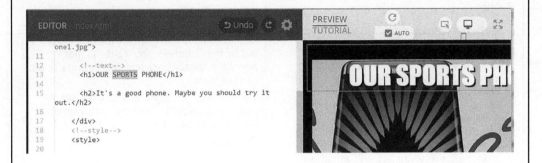

You will be given Mission cards to tell you what kind of changes to make in order to target specific Consumers.

If you get stuck you can access the following tutorial designed to help you change the image and text for the advert (click on the tutorial.html link). Make sure you save your work to publish it back into the Network. You should log into the system and click Publish.

Technical note on sharing

This last stage is only needed if you want to get a public version of these adverts on the internet. You may want to work out simpler ways of sharing, such as taking photographs of the screen with a tablet and sharing via a projector.

Mission cards

Once the demonstration has been carried out, set the Creatives to work using the mission cards, an example of which is given below. At the same time, circulate the following activity amongst the Consumers, without the Creatives knowing, and facilitate them starting to play with the technology accordingly to create 'subverts'. These are designed to deliberately undermine the intended impact of the original advert by poking fun at the product or including hidden messages about what the Network is up to.

(Continued)

(Continued)

Activity for Creatives	Activity for Consumers
The Network is demanding that all Creatives increase their output and try harder to target specific Consumers.	Keep this secret!
	You have found out that some of your friends have worked out a way to hack the messages of the Network.
Below are the most recent data on Consumer 0001.	Your activity is to take part in a hackathon, a way for subversive Consumers to crack the Network's code and alter the messages sent out by the Creatives. You'll publish these altered 'subverts' back into the Network so all can see them.
• Enjoys home baking • Has a robot dog	
You are required to create a personalised advert for the latest phone targeted at this Consumer. You need to add a background image that links the advert to your target's preferences. Give the phone a new name. How do you want your 'target' to feel when they see this phone? Add a tag line that will instantly capture your target's attention.	Through this, you hope to shock the people who run the Network and the Creatives who think they know it all.
	Good luck.

Once both Creatives and Consumers have had a chance to experiment, call the groups back together to share outcomes.

TIR as Network Spokesperson:

> Citizens, we would now like to share with you some of the Creatives' initial ideas. We would like you to view and assess each other's work in terms of its effectiveness in advertising to a target Consumer and ...

Alarm sound ... something has gone wrong with the Network!

TIR as Network Spokesperson panicked:

> Everyone stop what you are doing! It has come to our attention that the Network is being flooded by fake messages. We will now review the stream of messages and try to spot the difference between the fake messages and the legitimate, targeted ones.

Review and enjoy the messages created as a group. Once they have been reviewed and commented on the drama is over.

Out of role reflection

• What did we think of the subverts?
• Did we enjoy using the technology/software?

- What have we learned about using it?
- Are there similarities between how technology and data were used in the world of the drama and our own world?

Reflections on practice

Learning through drama is contingent and the manner in which this project will unfold will inevitably and productively vary according to context. However, below are a few issues that emerged from our experiences of running the drama with different groups, which we found particularly interesting.

Citizenship and control

The role of the Network Spokesperson was heavily influenced by modern day political practices around 'spin' and being 'on-message'. Following the Consumer/Creative divide, this was particularly useful in provoking strong reactions from participants around what the new system might entail for them on a personal level, such as the possibility of family separation. It is through such strong reactions that the drama works to connect and engage participants with the emerging issues, adding greater depth and meaning to what unfolds and what is produced. In one session, two close family members were separated from each other when the group divided into consumers and creatives and the resulting tension in the room was tangible until the drama was resolved.

Consumerism and identity

Interesting questions emerged around who got the better deal under the new system. While Consumers initially embraced opportunities to shop and spend, this shifted with the realisation that this was to be a continuous process and that the quality of the choices made would be 'assessed'. Similarly, Creatives quickly realised that the need to constantly create would quickly become exhausting. Both groups also resented the fact that the choice in how they live and consume had been taken away from them. Again, TIR as Network Spokesperson should be alert to opportunities to tap into these tensions and to stimulate participant responses to them.

The drama also provoked concern around the ecological cost of consumerism. What happens to all the 'stuff' the Consumers buy? Equally, is it actually necessary to produce physical objects or might the consuming be understood as a virtual process? Further questions arose in relation to the future of work that resonated with recent debates about automation and artificial intelligence. What will human beings do in a world in which they are no longer necessary to produce things? Will creativity and knowledge become the defining features of social organisation? Again, all of these issues tap into contemporary debates about who might be understood to constitute the new elites in our networked world and what happens to those of us who do not belong to this exclusive club.

Creative media production

A key message that emerged from the activity of creating internet memes was a celebration of the anarchic power of grass roots media creation. This formed a strong antidote to the repressive

(Continued)

(Continued)

atmosphere of the drama that had tracked and divided participants and we witnessed some great transformations as passive Consumers found their voices as rebel pranksters.

We are conscious that this activity requires a good deal of technical input and know-how. Working collaboratively with a technician is one way to manage this, if the teacher does not feel technically confident. We found developing the character of an assistant-in-role (AIR) enabled Mick to support the participants from within the drama. Indeed, 'Colin', as we named him, became integral to the unfolding narrative and provided an interesting contrast to the more sinister, controlling Network Spokesperson. Colin's more libertarian approach involved helping the Consumers to make their own media.

Hidden costs of free network services

This drama was planned and delivered before the Facebook and Cambridge Analytica media attention in 2018. However, the issue of data being used by companies to track and analyse behaviour did emerge in the exploration of this drama with more tech-savvy adult participants, and to a certain extent in our work with young people.

As we became more familiar with the drama and the tensions it provoked, we embraced challenges to 'The Network' that inevitably arose, and kept our responses to these deliberately vague, even unconvincing. For example, when participants raised concerns about the nature of the Creative/Consumer divide, we suggested it was set up for reasons of efficiency and that the technical nature of the Network was complex and beyond the understanding of everyday citizens. The reason for this less dogmatic approach was to provoke questioning around both the technology at play in organising the new society, and what might be the social, political and moral consequences of its application in this way.

It would be interesting to see if the drama could be developed or follow-up activities devised to better explore the hidden costs of free data services. For example, what are the implications of agreeing to terms of use we don't read? What is the political impact of the centralised control and distribution of information by ostensibly libertarian technology giants? What alternative strategies can we imagine together to allow us to become better data citizens?

CONCLUSION

We have illustrated ways in which drama can offer a mode of learning that is slow in comparison to the frenetic pace of school life and how this, in turn, can make concepts more relevant and meaningful. Drama encourages independence in the process of synthesising knowledge and experience. In drama we use the idea of being 'in role' as someone else to enable us to stretch the realms of possibility further. In other words, learners will still have opportunities to practise skills, test ideas, be critical thinkers, evaluate, plan and discover; the difference being that sometimes they will do it as themselves, and sometimes they will imagine they are someone else.

GLOSSARY OF DRAMA TECHNIQUES

LEARNERS IN ROLE

Learners are asked to take on roles other than themselves. They are given an occupation or specialism and asked to imagine what it might be like to be that person (see www.mantleoftheexpert.com/). The more detail that is created by the learner, the more likely they will be to engage with the idea and to accept the role-play. The time spent on investing in these roles is significant but has to be balanced with other lesson content.

TEACHER IN ROLE

The teacher manages and directs the drama from within. This allows the teacher to challenge attitudes or proposed actions from the point of view of his/her character. This is a very rewarding technique. If you have not previously used it, introduce it in short, tightly structured exercises. It does not need a great deal of acting ability; all it requires is the character to adopt a clear attitude either to others or to events. Use a 'role signifier' such as a hat or scarf to indicate clearly to the class when you are in role. When the role signifier is removed the class know you have returned to being teacher.

STILL IMAGE/FREEZE FRAME

A still dramatic image. This can either be specially created or produced by pausing a group or whole class role-play in mid-action. The tableau can represent a photograph, a statue, a memory or it can crystallise a moment, an idea or a theme. This allows participants to focus on a key moment of a narrative or can be used as a method of representing interesting or difficult content. Used in sequence they can be a very powerful and stylised way of telling a story, a dream sequence or nightmare. It can also be used to frame a piece of action giving a clear beginning and end when work is presented to the rest of the class.

THOUGHT-TRACKING

This reveals publicly the private thoughts/reactions of participants-in-role at specific moments in the action so as to develop a reflective attitude towards the action. This allows learners to consider characters more deeply as well as to analyse key moments in narrative. Action may be frozen and participants tapped on the shoulder for thoughts or thoughts may be prepared to go with the presentation of tableaux.

HOT SEATING

A participant (teacher or learner) sits on the 'hot seat'. This indicates that he/she is in role when on that seat. The rest of the group can then ask questions to the character. He/she must answer 'in role'. This highlights a character's attitude, motivation and personality. It can also develop a character before it is returned to the narrative. The more developed the context for 'hot seating' the better the quality of thought and response.

DEFINING THE SPACE

For whole class role-play, this strategy helps children to visualise the setting or location of the drama. This can be done very simply through the use of labels being placed in different areas of the room to indicate that location. For example, if the general location was a forest then labels could be placed to indicate where there is a pool, a path, the tall trees, a clearing, etc.

PRE-TEXT

Pre-text is an idea or proposition that acts as a catalyst for the drama. Examples of a pre-text could be a piece of text, a photograph or song lyrics. The term pre-text is used to describe the nature of a non-scripted collaborative enactment or what Cecily O'Neill (1995) describes as the 'source or impulse for the drama process . . . as well as indicating an excuse – reason for the work – it carries the meaning of text that exists before the event.'

REFERENCES

Anderson, M. (2012) *A Masterclass in Drama Education: Transforming Teaching and Learning.* London: Bloomsbury.

Anderson, M. (2014) The challenge of post-normality to drama education and applied theatre. *Research in Drama Education: The Journal of Applied Theatre and Performance,* 19(1), 110–120.

O'Neill, C. (1995) *Drama Worlds: A Framework for Process Drama.* Portsmouth, NH: Heinemann.

Rainer, J. & Lewis, M. (2012) *Drama at the Heart of the Secondary School: Projects to Promote Authentic Learning.* London: Routledge.

WEBSITE

Mantle of the Expert: www.mantleoftheexpert.com

8

ENGAGING GIRLS IN STEM

HELEN CALDWELL, SWAY GRANTHAM AND NEIL SMITH

The statistics on girls and women engaging in STEM at school and in the workplace are disappointing. Although the number of scientists increased globally by 5 million between 2000 and 2012, only a third of these scientists are women (UNESCO, 2016). In the UK, girls outperform or equal boys in A*-C (9-4) GCSE combined grades in all STEM subjects except mathematics. However, there follows a drop-off by the time they reach A levels, when all STEM subjects except biology have fewer female participants than male (Botcherby & Buckner, 2012). The fact that girls often do better than boys at school does not translate into the world of work, and in 2015 only 12.8% of the UK STEM workforce was female (WISE, 2014). Across the 34 OECD countries, less than 5% of girls think about pursuing a career in engineering and computing, and boys are four times as likely to consider STEM careers (OECD, 2015).

IN THIS CHAPTER

This chapter suggests that a STEM curriculum with 'girl appeal' builds upon relevant real world contexts and interests, makes the most of opportunities to add in aspects of the arts, and emphasises ways in which technology can support creative making and inventing. The chapter advocates a social constructivist pedagogy that values peer-led and shared learning. Our three activities incorporate these elements.

A recent OECD study found that girls lacked confidence in science and mathematics at school, and were reluctant to pursue careers in science and technology, even when they are academically successful in these subjects (OECD, 2015). This study also draws attention to a gender difference in girls' ability to 'think like scientists' and suggests that this is related to self-confidence. Students who are less cautious are more likely to persevere when faced with a challenge and to try out different solutions; these are important STEM skills. Reshma Saujani, founder of Girls Who Code, echoes this idea in her recent TED talk entitled 'Teach girls bravery, not perfection' (Saujani, 2016). Saujani points out that girls are often taught to play it safe and suggests that this may be why they gravitate towards careers in which they know they will succeed. In contrast, boys are taught to: 'play rough, swing high, crawl to the top of the monkey bars and then just jump off head first ... and by the time they are adults they're habituated to take risk after risk' (Saujani, 2016).

On a more positive note, there are many investigations and discussions about why this gender imbalance in the STEM workforce exists, and a wealth of recent initiatives that aim to address it by getting girls excited about STEM subjects. In the UK two social enterprises founded by Anne-Marie Imafidon and Mary Carty, Stemettes and Outbox Incubator, provide role models, run workshops and encourage girls to creatively explore science and technology through digital and physical making. Key to the success of these initiatives has been intensive mentoring, confidence building, networking and peer collaboration. Within a supportive community environment, girls become engaged with finding solutions to contemporary issues that have personal relevance. An overarching aim is to encourage girls to feel empowered to solve big problems.

A national outreach programme in the US, SciGirls, has combined a variety of research to suggest seven principles to engage girls in STEM (SciGirls, 2013):

1. Girls benefit from collaboration, especially when they can participate and communicate fairly.

2. Girls are motivated by projects they find personally relevant and meaningful.

3. Girls enjoy hands-on, open-ended projects and investigations.

4. Girls are motivated when they can approach projects in their own way, applying their creativity and unique talents.

5. Girls' confidence and performance improves in response to specific, positive feedback on things they can control, such as effort, strategies, and behaviours.

6. Girls gain confidence and trust in their own reasoning when encouraged to think critically.

7. Girls benefit from relationships with role models and mentors.

Taking these initiatives and recommendations into account, we suggest that the activities you plan for your classrooms should not be overtly 'girly'. Girls' perceptions of whether they are able to achieve in STEM can be negatively skewed by the idea that they need specifically female-friendly activities to succeed (Aspires Project, 2013), and as the SciGirls principles suggest, it is crucial that your pedagogy suits the variety of needs for learners in your class. It is also worth considering that many educators claim that the addition of an A for the Arts turning STEM into STEAM makes for a more powerful interaction between subjects (Robelen, 2011). An interdisciplinary approach that includes elements of design, creativity and real-world problem solving can provide an added attraction for girls. This way of working has much in common with the contemporary maker culture, which focuses on digital and physical tinkering with devices and materials, and is offering new and relevant ways into STEM.

—————— **ACTIVITY** ——————

Rescue Robots

What you need to know

This project provides a real-world context for STEM: how technology and science can help us reduce the casualties arising from natural disasters by designing prototype robots that can support human rescuers in a range of scenarios. Children think about the design features that make the robots suited to their activities and evaluate the effectiveness of their designs through testing. They use a 3D design app to refine their prototype design.

Testing is an important part of any science, technology and engineering project. However, when designing specialist equipment, such as that used for world disasters, it is unlikely that there will be regular testing scenarios. These industries must use simulations to allow them to replicate disasters as best they can. Simulations are part of the Computing, Science and D&T curriculums in the form of designing appropriate tests to evaluate end products.

The Oxford English Dictionary defines a robot as *'a machine capable of carrying out a complex series of actions automatically, especially one programmable by a computer'*. This is important as many children think that robots must look 'humanoid'.

Make sure that you have a range of different resources for the children to build their prototypes; the wider variety the better. Children must then focus on what is fit for purpose and not just *how* to use the tools you have given them.

Preparation

Objectives

To design, build and control a robot with a specific purpose.

Curriculum links

Computing: KS1 - create and debug simple programs; KS2 - design, write and debug programs that accomplish specific goals, including controlling or simulating physical systems.

Science: KS1 - performing simple tests; KS2 - using results to draw simple conclusions, make predictions for new values, suggest improvements and raise further questions.

Design and technology: KS1 - select from and use a wide range of materials and components, including construction materials, textiles and ingredients, according to their characteristics; KS2 - generate, develop, model and communicate their ideas through discussion, annotated sketches, cross-sectional and exploded diagrams, prototypes, pattern pieces and computer-aided design.

Year groups

All primary age children can tackle this activity - with curriculum differentiation as noted above.

(Continued)

(Continued)

Equipment

Floor robots (e.g. Bee-Bot, Blue-Bot, Probot, Roamer, Dash and Dot, Sphero), straws, card, paper, cardboard, junk modelling resources, string, glue, scissors, rulers, tracing paper, split pins, magnets, Sellotape.

Useful links

www.bbc.com/future/story/20140612-robots-to-the-rescue

http://spectrum.ieee.org/automaton/robotics/industrial-robots/japan-earthquake-more-robots-to-the-rescue

www.fastcoexist.com/1678731/six-rescue-robots-that-could-save-your-life/1

http://web-japan.org/trends/09_sci-tech/sci100909.html

www.popsci.com/tags/rescue-robots

http://crasar.org

Figure 8.1   Drones used as rescue robots

Setting the scene

Begin by discussing disasters with your class. Depending on their age, you may wish to start with fictional disasters occurring in familiar stories and TV programmes such as *Fireman Sam*, *Thunderbirds* or *The Powerpuff Girls*. Older children should be able to relate to real disasters and news stories such as the 9/11 attacks or the Fukushima nuclear disaster to reinforce the real world application of their ideas. Discuss the particular challenges of each rescue scenario and the risks to the rescuers.

You may find these links useful:

- www.bbc.co.uk/news/world-asia-india-35933452
- www.theguardian.com/world/2011/mar/11/japan-earthquake-miyagi-tsunami-warning
- http://news.bbc.co.uk/1/shared/spl/hi/uk/05/london_blasts/what_happened/html

Next, introduce the concept of robots being used to help with rescues. Discuss the purpose of a robot and how it can be suited to its role. Introduce children to the variety of robots that can be used in rescues, such as flying drones, mine rescue robots, snakebots that can slither through crevices, climbing robots or jointed robots that can navigate narrow spaces. Think about how some robots are designed with the characteristics of animals in mind, such as the slithering movement of a snake, the climbing ability of a gecko or the protective armour of a cockroach. Ask children to match images of robots to types of disasters and explain why they think that each robot is best suited to their activity. Look at the range of activities that might be carried out by the robots, including delivering food, air packs or medicine, assessing hazards, detecting survivors, conveying messages or taking photographs. Also consider the various ways in which robots are propelled and controlled, the range of sensors that can be attached to them and how they are designed to be durable and resistant to damage.

Trigger questions

- Why might robots be used in disasters?
- What can robots do that people can't?
- What features would a rescue robot need?
- What features would help a robot to guide the way?
- Could robots be used in water, fire or chemical based disasters?

Time to experiment: building the simulation

Group children in fours or fives. Give each group an image of a disaster to recreate in their area, ready for robot testing later. Ask children to assign each other roles based on their team's skills. The roles could be:

- Observer: scrutinises photographs of the disaster, suggesting what aspects they need to try and create.
- Resource manager: picks appropriate resources from the class supply and brings them to the group as necessary.
- Global viewer: keeps an eye on the whole picture and oversees everyone's role.
- Specific focus: focus on key elements of the disaster they are trying to create, e.g. one on the derailed train, another on the tree across the track.

Give the groups a time limit of around 15 minutes to create their environments. Remind them of the purpose of the activity and the need for realism. Next, children should briefly evaluate the strategies they employed to replicate different aspects of their environments.

(Continued)

(Continued)

Figure 8.2   Creating disaster scenarios

Adapting the robot

Depending on how familiar children are with using the robots, give them time to explore their robots' functions. Initially they may try controlling the robots on the floor and then move to the simulated environment, paying attention to their robot's capabilities and limitations. After this exploration time, children focus more closely on how their robot responds to their environment. They record their observations during the design, construction and testing phases and keep a photographic record of their work.

Next, we suggest starting to plan for structured sharing, with each child sharing their observations in turn, and then becoming more open. The result of this discussion will be an action plan of how to adapt their robot using the available materials to suit their environment. They will need to give thought to the purpose of their robot:

- Is it going to provide rescuers with a preview of the site only?
- Is it going to transport materials to a survivor?
- Is it going to pull survivors from a rescue site?

Figure 8.3   Planning robot adaptations

Designing a prototype

The next step is for children to build a modified robot that has additional features that enable it to complete the challenge. Again, make sure that the time limit is explicit. Prompt children to regularly test their customised robot designs as they develop; children have a natural tendency to wait until their work is finished to try it out, but this can mean a good deal of redoing if the initial ideas are not fit for purpose.

Disaster recovery

Each group presents what they have done and demonstrates their robot in action. Encourage explanations linking the properties of materials to the robot features that children have chosen to include and why they are necessary in their disaster environment. Peers will be able to help evaluate the designs' suitability for purpose as well as suggesting refinements for a second version. These discussions should also consider where ideas did not work and why some predictions did not come true. Children can often see things not working as a failure, but in STEM it is just one more thing you have found out: that *way* is not the *best* way to do it.

Also ask children to identify their own contributions so that they can all feel that their effort has been recognised. Aim to give them some specific feedback about how well they have engaged with the process of designing, testing and collaborating. The idea is to build understanding about the importance of trial and improve, and of persevering together to solve challenges. Focusing on the testing and prototype process rather than the product will give girls confidence to contribute their ideas and see them valued as part of the evolving solution.

Figure 8.4   Testing the prototypes

Final design challenge

As a final design challenge, children could use a CAD tool such as the free 123D Design iOS app or the free software by Autodesk to capture their refinements in a more professional-looking way. They will need to consider all that they have learned from the process so far, and reflect on the capabilities and limitations of their robot designs. They can revisit the designs of some existing and futuristic rescue robot prototypes. They might research some animal adaptations and think about how animals solve problems within their habitats.

(Continued)

(Continued)

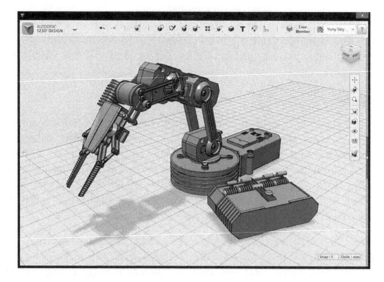

Figure 8.5 Final design challenge using 123D Design software or app

This final design may look nothing like the test robots but it does need to clearly demonstrate that it solves the original problem. Be sure to discuss the scientific, engineering, technological and mathematical reasons for the design decisions and discuss the differences between the different robots, the initial and customised designs, and the final rescue robot designs.

Review and reflect

- Why have you chosen those materials?
- What features were most important for a robot in your disaster? Why?
- How will your robot help human rescuers?
- What have you learned from your robot not being able to do certain things?
- What improvements or changes have you made from your initial design?

Assessment

While working on the activities, encourage self- and peer-assessment through discussions and evaluations linking back to the activity brief. These will focus children on the purpose of the activities and remind them that there is a real-world application for their designs.

Follow-up activities

Children could create an information leaflet that explains the purpose of the robot, what it does and instructions for how it works.

The 123D Design robots could be printed as models using a 3D printer.

Children can complete the Hazardous Duty Robots game from STEMWorks, which involves assigning the right robot to deal with three scenarios: a terrorist bomb threat, a land mine patrol and a nuclear disaster (see http://stem-works.com/external/activity/164).

Further robotics STEM activities can be found at http://stem-works.com/subjects/1-robotics/activities

ACTIVITY

Oil Chaos

What you need to know

This activity involves cleaning oil from a pool of water. Oil spills often take years to clean up for two main reasons. First, there is so much water for the oil to spread over. Second, oil is hydrophobic which means it hates water and will try to attach itself to anything that is not water, e.g. wildlife, rocks and people.

When oil spills happen, environmentalists try to fix the mess by:

1. Skimming oil from the water surface (oil floats)
2. Absorbing the oil (encouraging the oil to stick to giant sponges)
3. Adding a dispersant (like a detergent, to break up the oil)

This project enables children to recreate these methods of cleaning oil spills.

Preparation

Objectives

To understand how to separate materials.

Curriculum links

Science: skills of observations, predictions, hypotheses, conclusions; properties of materials.

Year groups

Years 4-6.

Equipment

Cooking oil mixed with black food colouring, buckets of water, disposable gloves, sponges, paper towels, kitchen roll, plastic spoons, feathers, rocks and pebbles, 'grease fighting' dishwashing

(Continued)

(Continued)

detergent, measuring cylinders, sieves, tea strainers, blotting paper and any other separating equipment that you can find in the science cupboards.

Useful links

www.mnn.com/earth-matters/wilderness-resources/stories/the-13-largest-oil-spills-in-history

www.houstonchronicle.com/opinion/outlook/article/The-Gulf-Coast-from-disaster-to-opportunity-7468157.php

www.bbc.co.uk/news/10309001

Setting the scene

Show children news articles about oil spills and ask them why there is oil in the sea. Ensure they understand that we drill oil from under the sea and that sometimes the pipes or seals leak. Point out that large ships, which use oil as fuel, can crash and that this can also cause an oil leak. Think about predicting the consequences of such events. Discuss what children already know about the short-term and longer-term effects of oil spills and what we can do to fix the problem.

Figure 8.6   Oil rig explosion

Trigger questions

- How does the oil get into the sea?
- Why is it a problem if oil gets into the sea?
- What can people do about oil in the sea?
- Can you suggest any ways clean-up crews could get rid of the oil?
- What equipment might they need?

Time to experiment

To begin with, children have a small amount of water with oil in it and in pairs they experiment with the resources to hand. They need to find out what is effective and imagine how the problem might be different on a larger scale. In this initial stage, there should just be an empty tray of oily water, but in the ongoing project there will be objects in the water, such as feathers and rocks and they need to consider how they will clean them.

This experiential time is crucial to allow children to recognise each tool's use and the pros and cons of each method. Encourage the children to spend some time using sequences of approaches, as it is unlikely that they will find just one tool that will do the job. Enable children to record what they have found out while experimenting and think about using digital tools that offer media options such as Explain Everything, iMovie, Book Creator or Thinglink to create a shareable digital artefact that represents their learning.

Trial and improve

Group children into teams and ask them to share findings. Collectively, they should hypothesise what they think the best approach might be, giving reasons to justify their answers. These ideas could be shared in a class discussion to model the process of collective problem solving.

Next, give each group of children a full container of water that includes a stone, a feather and a measured quantity of oil. Equipment should be laid out clearly but not given to specific groups so that children can decide what scientific tools they need and in what order they want to use them. Ask children to assign themselves to roles such as:

- Observers – what is happening?
- Predictors – what will happen next? Is it time to change plan?
- Resource managers – what other equipment could we use? What should we exchange?

These roles could be rotated during the activity to allow children to develop and reflect upon each skill.

During this stage, children should apply what they have learned about effective oil clean-ups and try different combinations of tools and techniques. After some time, stop the groups and ask them to evaluate the effectiveness of their strategies. How much cleaner is the water? The groups could then compare the volume of oil in their bucket to the other groups and share the effectiveness of their procedures.

(Continued)

(Continued)

Finally, the groups should look at the effect of the oil on their feathers and rocks. They should once again compare results and share successes and challenges. Your discussion can link this back to the real-world objects they represent, with the rock representing land, beaches, solid objects in the sea, and the feather representing birds and wildlife.

Communicating learning

To consolidate their understanding, children could add to their digital artefact information about oil leaks including their scientific understanding of why oil spills are difficult to clear up and what methods environmentalists have at their disposal. They should explain equipment and methods that can be engineered to help clean up oil spills and then outline the process they went through in clearing the oil from the water in their buckets.

Review and reflect

- Why is it so difficult to get the water out of the oil?
- Why is an oil spill dangerous to animals?
- What methods do environmentalists use to clear the water?
- What does absorption mean?
- Why does it take so long to clean up oil spills?
- What can we do to help oil spill clean ups?

Assessment

Teachers can assess scientific understanding through the discussions and the recording of observations and predictions. They can also use modelling and guiding to encourage children to develop their initial ideas. Rotating roles within teams encourages children to self-assess as they 'hand over' and reflect on what they would do differently in the role next time.

Follow-up activities

Children might create news reports about a fictional oil spill and explain what environmentalists are doing to try and fix the problem. You could use green screen techniques to make a newscast. This can be simple to achieve using a green PowerPoint slide or some backing paper, a mobile device and the app Greenscreen by DoInk.

Oil painting techniques could be explored using water-soluble oil paints, and the challenge of cleaning brushes and hands when using traditional oil paints researched and related to existing knowledge about the materials from the project.

Digital artefacts recording project outcomes can be shared with the wider school community.

ACTIVITY

What Does Your House Look Like?

What you need to know

In this activity, children build a shelter following the 'Design, Make, Evaluate' process suggested in the Design and Technology programmes of study. This process could be repeated more than once with children refining their ideas during each iteration.

Preparation

Objectives

To use a range of materials to build a shelter.

Curriculum links

D&T: design, make, evaluate.

Science: materials and their properties.

Mathematics: measurement.

Year groups

Years 1 and 2.

Equipment

Twigs, logs, moss, grass, black bags, string, tape, scissors, paper, newspaper, cotton wool.

Setting the scene

Teachers could introduce this project using the book *Let's Build a House* (Manning & Granström, 2014). This is the fun tale of a boy who imagines lots of different houses and what they could look like. It could provide an impetus for the class to think about planning their own shelters. You might introduce some characters, perhaps classroom teddies, dolls or Lego people who need somewhere to live. The children's challenge is to build them suitable houses.

During this experimental time, children create their own list of 'must, should and could' features for a structure. This enables them to take ownership of their learning and allows for a more open-ended activity for those who find the challenge difficult.

Trigger questions

*   Why do we need houses?
*   What do houses look like?

(Continued)

(Continued)

Figure 8.7   Prototype designs for sustainable shelters

- What could we use to build shelters?
- Is there anything we can find around the classroom to help us?
- Why would we choose this material?

Time to experiment

Rather than just giving the children a range of resources they might need, it can be beneficial to collect and find resources. Encourage children to list useful resources such as paper, tape, sticks or string together as a group and then send them to find them around the classroom. This shows children that they can continue to add to their resources by using other things around the classroom.

Design

Lay all the resources out in one place and ask children to suggest how they could use them. Encourage them to justify their answers by thinking about the properties of the materials, for example why would paper not work if it rained?

Ask children to draw and label their ideas, annotating their designs with questions (How will it stand?) and tests (How can I make a stick stand upright?). They will need to try out their structural ideas to discover why some work and others do not. Once they have the basic structure sorted, children can consider the materials they will use to create their shelter. This is a good time to link to the previous discussion of the properties of materials and children should incorporate this into their notes. Depending on the ages that you are working with, you might encourage children to put some approximate measurements on their plans as well.

Make

Before embarking on the 'make' stage of the process, you will need to ensure that the ground rules are explicit. What resources should children not use in their shelters? Also, talk to them about wastage and cutting out shapes near the edge rather than in the centre of a piece of paper. This should avoid having to interrupt children when they are in the flow of making their creations. Give them a time limit, which ideally you can show visually, such as by using a website-based sand timer. This allows your learners to begin to regulate their own time.

Small groups work best for this activity as it allows each child to feel their contribution is valued. While working in pairs or trios, children can help each other out without having too many differing ideas and the complications of trying to please everyone.

The role of the teacher during this time is to facilitate specific learning on the theme of forces and structures in the context of children's practical problem solving. This could be by making suggestions about strengthening techniques, such as using triangles in the corners, to help children realise their ideas.

Evaluate

Once the time is up, allow children time to present their shelter to the class. Invite them to explain their choices, what they did and, most importantly, why they did it. These presentations provide a structured opportunity for self-evaluation as children reflect on what they have achieved and what they would like to improve given more time. They also provide opportunities for peer assessment where other children can suggest what they like and what they think could be improved.

Finally, children should refer to the list of 'must, should, could' that they made in the beginning and make final judgements about the effectiveness of their shelter and its suitability for purpose.

Review and reflection questions

- What does an effective shelter need?
- Which materials were most useful in our shelter?
- How did we strengthen our shelter?
- What shapes created the best shelters?

Assessment

During the design stage, children's initial annotated designs can provide assessment information about their understanding of design and technology structures, the scientific properties of materials and their mathematical understanding of measurements. During the make stage, the teacher can discuss the choices children have made and use this as formative assessment. Children self- and peer assess during the evaluation stage through their presentations. Their confidence in their explanations can be assessed by the teacher.

Follow-up activities

Children could explore what different shelters and homes look like around the world. They could explore structures such as wigwams, treehouses and rainforest shelters and explain the differences in choice of materials, structural designs and building methods.

(Continued)

(Continued)

The home and shelter designs could prompt drama, animation and digital storytelling, and a range of media techniques might be used to capture and share the results, promoting the idea of STEM to STEAM. Useful apps include iMovie, Greenscreen by Do Ink, I Can Animate, Book Creator, Puppet Pals HD Directors Pass and Shadow Puppets Edu.

DISCUSSION

These three projects were designed to align with the SciGirls' seven principles for how to engage girls in STEM. The project designs relate to the first three principles: they are open-ended; they concern real-world situations to which the children can relate; and the activities are carried out in small groups to encourage collaboration and communication.

Application of the next four principles depends on the teacher. We have suggested that children are encouraged to approach the activities in their own way, even though the overall aim is known. The frequent opportunities for testing and evaluation encourages critical thinking. The investigative nature of the activities gives opportunities for specific feedback about learning behaviours, and we would encourage teachers to cultivate a prescriptive style of feedback that focuses on the strategies children use during the learning process (Halpern et al., 2007). The aim is to strengthen girls' beliefs about their own abilities, and improve their persistence and performance when undertaking challenge-based learning. Another important consideration is the need to provide girls with role models and mentors.

Teaching strategies that require children to explain how they solved a problem, apply what they have learned outside the classroom and work more independently have been shown to improve results for girls (OECD, 2015). And the outstanding message from initiatives such as SciGirls, Girls Who Code, Stemettes and Outbox Incubator is that teaching that is good for girls is good for all learners and we should all aim for inclusive practices. Our projects have shown how STEM learning experiences can be structured to be engaging for all children. Presenting problem-based collaborative activities, with learning and technology embedded, can be stimulating for all learners. The projects, and the real-world challenges they relate to, can act as a hook for children during other learning experiences. All children benefit from active learning experiences that they can easily relate to their interests or experience. And all children benefit from gaining confidence in their thinking skills.

There are some actions that parents, carers and teachers can take to nurture and champion girls' engagement with STEM.

We suggest that teachers:

- Aim to get across the excitement of working in STEM and choose activities that spark girls' interest and curiosity.

- Encourage girls to have the confidence to think outside the box through problem solving and risk taking.

- Use questioning carefully to help girls feel comfortable about exploring and experimenting.

- Make sure that girls have an equal voice to boys in the classroom and address gender differences in self-confidence.

- Build a supportive network of peers and adopt teaching styles that encourage collaboration so that girls gain a sense of belonging in a field in which they can work together.

- Be aware that STEM is a combination of hard and soft skills, and teach girls to keep trying when faced with a challenge.

- Open girls' minds to their own talents and to possible future careers, and help them to understand that they can achieve through effort.

- Be aware of the social and emotional dimensions of STEM learning; be sensitive to cultural pressures and talk about how to handle the unconscious gender biases that girls might encounter.

- Build a positive image of women in STEM and challenge stereotypes by exposing girls to role models through field trips to STEM workplaces, exemplar biographies, reference to current events and guest speakers (e.g. STEM ambassadors).

- Provide access to rich and engaging sources of information and use technology to create shareable project outputs for authentic audiences.

- Promote engagement by incorporating the arts into STEM teaching and integrating subjects through STEAM.

And we suggest that teachers encourage parents and carers to:

- Take a similar view to building positive images of women in STEM.

- Provide girls with early technology and computing experiences, and give girls opportunities to play with construction kits such as Lego and Meccano.

- Provide ongoing encouragement in girls' engagement in STEM subjects.

- Give their sons and daughters equal support in STEM career aspirations.

In conclusion, there is nothing inherently gendered about any subject in the STEM field. Achieving gender parity in STEM will contribute to the economic security of women and their families, and to the economic growth of their societies around the world. It will help ensure that girls achieve their potential and that we bring girls' talents into our national pool of innovation and creativity. When all children see STEM subjects as accessible and relevant to real world problems that they care about, and believe they can make genuine contributions, they will engage more deeply. And when primary-aged girls see that they can succeed with STEM subjects, they will have the confidence to continue with them later, if that is where their interests lie. As Reshma Saujani says in her TED talk (Saujani, 2016):

> We have to teach them to be brave in schools and early in their careers, when it has the most potential to impact their lives and the lives of others, and we have to show them that they will be loved and accepted not for being perfect but for being courageous.

REFERENCES

Aspires Project. (2013) *The case for early education about STEM careers*. Available at www.kcl.ac.uk/sspp/departments/education/research/aspires/ASPIRESpublications.aspx (accessed 29 May 2016).

Botcherby, S. & Buckner, L. (2012) *Women in Science, Technology, Engineering and Mathematics: from Classroom to Boardroom: UK Statistics 2012*. Leeds: WISE.

Halpern, D., Aronson, J., Reimer, N., Simpkins, S., Star, J. & Wentzel, K. (2007) *Encouraging Girls in Math and Science* (NCER 2007-2003). Washington, DC: National Center for Education Research, Institute of Education Sciences, US Department of Education.

Manning, M. & Granström, B. (2014) *Let's Build a House: A Book about Buildings and Materials*. London: Franklin Watts.

OECD. (2015) *The ABC of Gender Equality in Education: Aptitude, Behaviour Confidence*. Paris: OECD Publishing.

Robelen, E. W. (2011) *STEAM: experts make case for adding arts to STEM*. Available at www.edweek.org/ew/articles/2011/12/01/13steam_ep.h31.html (accessed 29 May 2016).

Saujani, R. (2016) *Teach girls bravery, not perfection TED Talk*. Available at www.ted.com/talks/reshma_saujani_teach_girls_bravery_not_perfection (accessed 29 May 2016).

SciGirls. (2013). *SciGirls seven: how to engage girls in STEM*. Available at http://scigirlsconnect.org/page/scigirls-seven (accessed 29 May 2016).

UNESCO. (2016) Institute for Statistics Data Centre. Available at http://uis.unesco.org (accessed May 2016).

WISE (2014) *Women in Science, Technology, Engineering and Mathematics: The Talent Pipeline from Classroom to Boardroom: UK Statistics 2014*. Leeds: WISE.

FURTHER READING

Ashcraft, C., Eger, E. & Friend, M. (2012) *Girls in IT: The facts*. Boulder, CO: National Center for Women & Information Technology.

Chatman, L., Nielsen, K., Strauss, E. J. & Tanner, K. D. (2008) *Girls in Science: A Framework for Action*. Arlington, VA: NSTA Press, National Science Teachers Association.

Freedman, K. & Stuhr, P. (2004) Curriculum change for the 21st century: visual culture in art education. In E. W. Eisner & M. D. Day (eds), *Handbook of Research and Policy in Art Education*. London: Routledge, pp. 815-828.

Parker, L. H. & Rennie, L. J. (2002) Teachers' implementation of gender inclusive instructional strategies in single-sex and mixed-sex science classrooms. *International Journal of Science Education*, 24(9), 881-897.

WEBSITES

National Girls Collaborative Project: Engaging Girls in STEM: https://ngcproject.org/engaging-girls-stem

Practical Action: STEM challenges in schools: http://practicalaction.org/challengesinschools

9
COMPUTING AND STEM

YASEMIN ALLSOP

Our understanding of how people learn has developed substantially over the years. We now know that in order for people to learn, the learner has to be both at the centre of the learning experience and also have opportunities to make connections across disciplines. The traditional way of teaching subjects in isolation is not the best way of teaching children. They need to learn the same material in different contextual settings. STEM gives children opportunities to investigate an idea in different contexts. For example, using the Scratch visual coding program children can learn to code, but if they create a circuit using Scratch they learn about electricity and circuits at the same time. Learning in this way becomes more relevant to students and they can practise skills such as creating and testing ideas, making predictions, critical thinking, evaluation and planning.

IN THIS CHAPTER

The three activities in this chapter demonstrate the strong coherence between computing, mathematics, science and engineering. Using a project-based learning (PBL) approach these activities give control to children allowing them to learn at their own pace.

STEM education aims to blend scientific inquiry and technological design process through PBL that focuses on developing learners' critical thinking, problem solving, logical reasoning, technical, communication, collaboration, self-directing and creativity skills. Figure 9.1 presents the STEM skills. Although the subjects included under the umbrella of STEM can vary in different countries, mathematics, biology, chemistry, computer science, electronics, communications and mechanical engineering are mainly identified as the STEM disciplines.

It is often said that computer science is the silent 'C' in STEM as it contributes to the development of the many valuable skills in all of the STEM disciplines (science, technology, engineering, mathematics). For example, the problem-solving process, which is integral to learning in all of the STEM fields, follows a very similar trail in all domains. In mathematics, students start by understanding the problem, they design a means of

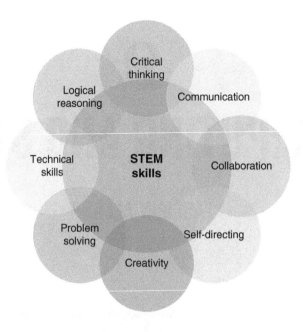

Figure 9.1 STEM skills

solution and apply this to achieve a solution, sometimes using technology such as computers or calculators; finally they evaluate their solution in the context of the original problem. Similarly, in science, children start by setting up the problem, they think about ways of solving the problem and investigate different solutions by testing their ideas. Finally, when they complete their investigations, they share, discuss and come up with conclusions. In programming, learners start by understanding the activity and what they need to accomplish, in other words the problem. They design an algorithm to achieve the specific activity and then write code for the computer to realise the solution. They test their code, to make sure that it works and debug errors as they occur. They share their program with their friends and discuss the effectiveness of their solution. In many ways coding can be seen as applied mathematics and science as it provides a context for learners to solve problems using the iterative approach, meaning they can achieve the desired outcome by repeating the cycle of operations. Thus computer science can be seen as a STEM discipline.

ACTIVITY

Mathematics through Scratch

What you need to know

Scratch is a freely available web based visual coding application. While working on mathematics activities using Scratch, children learn about selection, sequence, repetition and they work with variables. They drag and drop Scratch code blocks to write their own programs to achieve a specific objective. They debug problems and share their work online, so they can receive comments that will help them to celebrate their achievements and improve their work further.

It is vital that children experiment with the Scratch program for a while before introducing the activity. Children should also revise their understanding of the properties of 2D polygons and how to calculate their perimeter.

Preparation

Objectives

Create a program to draw 2D shapes.

Design and write a program that calculates the perimeter of 2D shapes.

Curriculum links

Computing: design, write and debug programs that accomplish specific goals.

Mathematics: identify and draw 2D shapes, calculate the perimeter of 2D shapes.

Year groups

Years 4, 5 and 6, older children could find area as well as perimeter.

Equipment

Computer, Scratch program, pen, paper, small bag or a box.

Useful links

https://scratch.mit.edu

http://scratched.gse.harvard.edu/resources/vector-scratch-blocks

https://scratch.mit.edu/info/cards/

http://drscratch.programamos.es

Setting the scene

Explain to children that they will design and write two programs for the computer to execute using the 'Scratch' application. The first program will make the computer draw 2D shapes and the second will calculate the perimeter of the 2D shapes.

Write the properties of 2D shapes onto small cards and place these in a small bag or a box. Ask a child to select one card from the bag and to read aloud the properties of a shape. Can they guess what shape this is? How can you calculate the perimeter of this shape? Repeat this activity a few more times.

Stand in front of a white board with a pen in your hand. Ask the children to give you instructions to draw a square. Discuss their instructions; how specific were they? Did they use mathematical vocabulary when they were giving their instructions to you? Could they have used fewer instructions?

Repeat the activity above using hands-on Scratch coding blocks, which you can download from http://scratched.gse.harvard.edu/resources/vector-scratch-blocks. Discuss the purpose of 'Pen down' and 'Pen up'. Remind the children that they need to start with an execution code to run

(Continued)

(Continued)

their program such as: 'When I click on the green flag', 'When I click on the sprite'. Let them pro-gram each other using 'Scratch' coding blocks to draw different 2D shapes.

Trigger questions

What do 'Pen down' and 'Pen up' code blocks do?

What are the steps for drawing a square?

What coding blocks can you use to execute your program?

How can you draw a square using fewer code blocks?

Can you write a program using Scratch blocks for calculating the perimeter of a rectangle? Discuss with your partner.

Time to experiment

Introduce the children to the Scratch interface. Model how to drag and drop the code blocks to write a simple program. Let them explore the program with their partner. Give them simple activities such as: add a sound, add another sprite, make a sprite glide across the screen. You can provide

Table 9.1   How to draw a square?

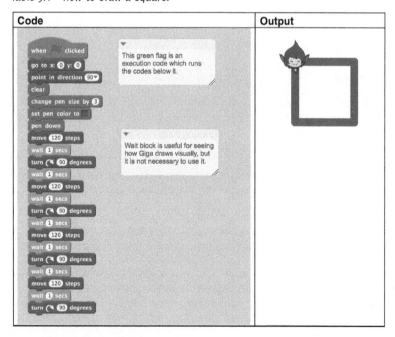

Code	Output
when [green flag] clicked go to x: 0 y: 0 point in direction 90 clear change pen size by 3 set pen color to [ ] pen down move 120 steps wait 1 secs turn ↻ 90 degrees wait 1 secs move 120 steps wait 1 secs turn ↻ 90 degrees wait 1 secs move 120 steps wait 1 secs turn ↻ 90 degrees wait 1 secs move 120 steps wait 1 secs turn ↻ 90 degrees This green flag is an execution code which runs the codes below it. Wait block is useful for seeing how Giga draws visually, but it is not necessary to use it.	

them with Scratch Cards to learn how to code with Scratch. They can be downloaded from https://scratch.mit.edu/info/cards

Tell the children they will be teaching their sprite how to draw a square on the stage. Can they come up with a code for their sprite to draw a square? Let them try and share their ideas.

Display Table 9.1, which shows the basic program for drawing a square. Can they think of another way of writing this program using fewer codes? Let them work with their partners and allow them to give their feedback to the whole class.

Display Table 9.2 and let the children compare this with their solution. Can they edit their code to draw different 2D shapes, such as a triangle? What do they need to change? Will the angle stay as 90 degrees? Did knowing the properties of a triangle help them when they were writing their codes?

Table 9.2   Drawing a square using 'Repeat' function

Code	Output
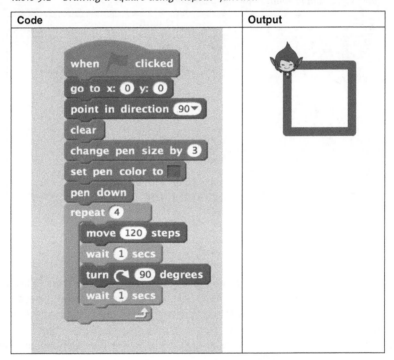	

Bring the bag that contains the cards with the properties of 2D shapes written on them. Let them choose a card; identify the shape from given properties and then write a program for their sprite to draw their selected shape.

(Continued)

(Continued)

Ask the children how to find the perimeter of a shape - make sure they understand it is the total distance around the shape.

Ask the children how to calculate the perimeter of a rectangle. Can they write a formula using Scratch codes for their sprite to calculate the perimeter of a rectangle? Let them work in pairs and share their work with their partner. It is useful to provide children with a tool to keep a record of their problem-solving activities, e.g. camera, tablet, diary.

Display the example solution (Table 9.3) on the board and ask the children to compare it with their codes. Did they use variables for length, width and perimeter?

Can you edit your code to calculate the perimeter of a square? Equilateral triangle?

Table 9.3 Example solution for the perimeter

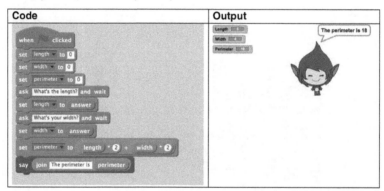

Review and reflect

Providing children with a tool such as a camera, tablet or a diary will help them to keep a record of their problem-solving activities. They can either take photographs or create videos of their code that doesn't work. They can share this with their peers or the whole class to reflect on and discuss possible solutions. They can also keep a written record of their problems either in text or picture format. It is important that children have time to stop and review their work either independently or with their peers, depending on the activity.

Children should discuss:

- How they designed their solutions.
- What strategies they used for debugging errors and how they selected them.
- What improvements or changes they made to their initial programs.

Assessment

You could provide children with a list of success criteria at the beginning of the project, enabling them to either evaluate their work independently or with their partners. It is important to involve them when setting the criteria. You could include both closed- and open-questions such as: Did you test your program? Did it work? If not, how did you solve the problem? What strategies did you use? Were you able to write your program using fewer coding blocks?

Follow-up activities

Children could write a formula using Scratch codes for their sprite to calculate the area of polygons.

ACTIVITY

Birthday Card Circuits

This project is inspired by Kim Wilkens, founder of Tech-Girls. You can find many amazing projects on her website: http://makerprojects.wikispaces.com/papercircuits

What you need to know

In this project, children will learn about electric circuits through making a card with LEDs for an occasion (e.g. Christmas, birthday, Mother's Day). They will investigate how a circuit works and use this information to create a basic electric circuit and turn on an LED light on either cardstock paper or felt. They will first create their card and then decorate it using different materials and LED lights. They will learn about Boolean Logic, a type of data with two values: 'true' or 'false'.

Preparation

Objectives

- Know how electrical circuits and components can be used to create functional products.
- Plan the main stages of making.
- Cut and shape materials accurately.
- Assemble materials and components accurately.
- Critically evaluate the quality of the design for the intended purpose.

Curriculum links

Design and technology: create a step-by-step plan for making. Accurately cut and assemble materials. Evaluate designs and check whether they are fit for purpose.

(Continued)

(Continued)

Computing: Boolean logic, logic gates as an electric circuit with two inputs and one output. Keep a record of activity and present as a blog or wiki.

Art: design and create using different materials, e.g. paper, felt.

Science: construct a simple electronic circuit using LEDs, aluminium tape and battery.

Year groups

Years 4, 5 and 6.

Equipment

Felt, colouring pens, paper, cardstock paper, 3V coin batteries, aluminium tape, masking tape and LEDs.

Useful links

https://youtu.be/js7Q-r7G9ug

www.kidblog.org

www.wikispaces.com

www.weebly.com

Setting the scene

Let the children explore Electrical Circuits on some websites:

www.bbc.co.uk/bitesize/ks2/science/physical_processes/electrical_circuits/read/1/

www.learningcircuits.co.uk

Ask the children what a circuit needs (power source, e.g. battery and wires connected to both the positive and negative sides of the battery; it can also have different components such as LEDs, motors).

Display some incomplete circuit images and ask the children to identify the problem. Let them discuss in groups and get feedback from each group.

Allow the children to play electrical circuits games on BBC sites:

www.bbc.co.uk/bitesize/ks2/science/physical_processes/electrical_circuits/play/

www.bbc.co.uk/schools/scienceclips/ages/10_11/changing_circuits.shtml

Model how to write a blog post using a blogging site, e.g. Kidblog or Wikispaces. Ask the children to reflect on what they learned from the websites visited and the games played in a blog post. Explain they must keep a record of their work on their blogs. They can use images, videos or text to share their work.

Trigger questions

What is an electrical circuit?

What do you need to build a complete circuit?

Why are electrical wires covered with plastic or rubber?

Why might a circuit fail to work?

What symbol represents a battery in a circuit?

Time to experiment

Ask the children to practise drawing basic circuits on a sheet of paper. Is it a complete circuit? How could they test it?

Let the children design their cards using cardstock paper, felt or both. They need to make a small hole, through which to place the LED. At the back of the card, on each side of the hole place a piece of aluminium tape. Mark one piece of the aluminium tape as positive (+) and the other as negative (-).

Push the LED through the hole. Make sure that the shorter leg of the LED is taped to the negative aluminium tape and that the longer leg of the LED is taped to the positive aluminium tape.

Use a tiny piece of masking tape to stick the battery positive side down to the positive aluminium tape; make sure the battery is not covered.

To complete the circuit, run aluminium tape from the battery to the negative aluminium tape.

Review and reflect

Ask the children to evaluate each other's cards.

Can they test their friends' circuit to make sure that it works?

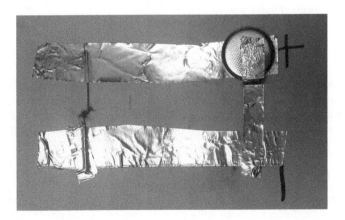

(Continued)

(Continued)

Can they think of reasons why their circuits may have a problem?

Were the design and materials used appropriately for the activity?

Were the materials assembled correctly?

How could their friend improve their design?

Can they give verbal feedback to their friend?

Assessment

The children can take photographs of each step as it is completed, or create a video as they make their card. They can upload these and share them using tools such as blogs (www.kidblog.org) or wikispaces (www.wikispaces.com). The children can visit each other's blogs and leave comments. They need to write one positive comment, one point for an improvement and then another positive comment.

Follow-up activities

Ask the children to come up with another power source instead of a battery. Give them a Raspberry Pi or an Arduino. Can they write a simple program using either Scratch or Python to light the LED?

ACTIVITY

Spinning Planets

This activity is inspired by the 'Spinning flower' activity from the Raspberry Pi learning resources team: https://projects.raspberrypi.org/en/projects/spinning-flower-wheel

You can find many other fabulous activities on their website: www.raspberrypi.org/resources/.

What you need to know

In this activity the children will learn to write a simple program using Python to control a motor using Raspberry Pi and breadboard. They will work with procedures and variables. They will learn about the characteristics of the planets and use this information to create a 3D model of the solar system.

Preparation

Objectives

- Write a simple program to program a motor to spin forwards and backwards.
- Research and compare the characteristics of different planets.
- Perform simple tests.
- Plan the main stages of making.
- Assemble materials and components accurately.
- Critically evaluate the quality of the design for its intended purpose.

Curriculum links

Science: the solar system.

Computing: programming a motor using a physical system (Raspberry Pi).

Design and technology: create a step-by-step plan as a guide for making. Accurately cut and assemble materials. Evaluate designs and check whether they are fit for purpose.

Year groups

Years 4, 5 and 6.

Equipment

A paper cup, coloured pen and paper to create planets or pictures of planets, glue, scissors, Raspberry Pi, one wheel, one geared motor, male to male jumper leads, HDMI cable, screen for Raspberry Pi.

Useful links

Make a digital garden with Pibrella and Raspberry Pi by Geek Gurl Diaries: www.youtube.com/watch?v=4Fs7y7gZlag

(Continued)

(Continued)

Solar system class clips: www.bbc.co.uk/education/topics/zdrrd2p/resources/1

Information on planets:

www.planetsforkids.org

www.kidsastronomy.com/solar_system.htm

https://youtu.be/Qd6nLM2QIWw

Resources supporting STEM learning: www.stem.org.uk

Setting the scene

Explain to the children that they will be creating spinning planets with a wheel and a motor that can be programmed using a Raspberry Pi, a credit-card-sized computer.

Ask them to visit different websites on the internet to find out about the solar system and the characteristics of the planets (e.g. size, how far from the Earth). Let the children draw the planets on a sheet of paper and colour them. It might be useful to discuss the solar system and relative positions of the planets in the solar system.

Trigger questions

Which planet is closest to the Sun?

The sixth planet from the Sun features an extensive ring system. What is the name of this planet?

What is a Raspberry Pi?

How do you attach the motor to the Raspberry Pi? Can you explain?

Can you write a sequence to move the motor in different directions?

Can you make the motor go slower?

Time to experiment

Explain to the children that their activity is to write a simple program to move the motor forward and/or backwards using Python or Raspberry Pi.

Demonstrate how to make the motor move and let the children explore it for themselves. Can they create a sequence for the motor to move? (See the Appendix.) Can they make it faster? Slower?

Let them assemble the motor to Paper cup and the wheel.

Attach the motor and wheels to the Explorer hat on the Raspberry Pi using male-to male jumpers.

Finally let the children write their code to make the planet spin round.

Review and reflect

Can the children test their code to make sure that it works and help each other to debug any errors they identify? Let them discuss how they debugged the problems. Can they place their planet in the correct position to create a model of the solar system?

Let them compare and evaluate their own design and others'. Did they use a similar code sequence to make their motor move?

Assessment

Let children take a photograph of each step as it is completed and share it in their blog. They can use freely available programs such as kidblog.org or wikispaces.com. They can also write posts to reflect on the process of making their design.

Follow-up activities

Make a model of the solar system by creating different planets.

Change the speed of the motor.

Can they add sound?

FURTHER READING

Allsop, Y. & Sedman, B. (2015) *Primary Computing in Action*. London: John Catt Educational.

Barton, D., Farrell, D. & Mourshed, M. (2014) *Education to Employment: Designing a System That Works*. New York: McKinsey Center for Government.

Caprile, M. et al. (2015) *Encouraging STEM studies for the Labour Market*. Study for the EMPL Committee. Brussels: European Union.

Intel Corporation. (2015) *Increasing Employability and Accelerating Economic Growth Worldwide*. Available at www.intel.com/content/dam/www/public/us/en/documents/brief/innovation-for-employability-brief.pdf

National Math + Science Initiative. (2014) *The STEM Crisis*. Available at www.nms.org/Portals/0/Docs/STEM%20Crisis%20Page%20Stats%20and%20References.pdf

APPENDIX

PYTHON CODE TO USE WITH THE SPINNING PLANETS ACTIVITY

You can use the Explorer hat or Pibrella board for this activity.

FOR USING WITH PIBRELLA

After assembling the wheel and motor attach it to Pibrella. Begin with importing the Pibrella and time python library. Then leave a line empty by pressing enter. Then add the code to control the motor. Save your code and run it.

```
import pibrella
import time

pibrella.output.e.on()
time.sleep (5)
pibrella.output.e.off()
```

FOR USING WITH THE EXPLORER HAT

First install the library via the terminal using the code below:

```
sudo curl get.pimoroni.com/explorerhat | bash
```

Then use the following code to control the motor:

```
import explorerhat
import time

explorerhat.motor.one.forwards(100)
time.sleep (duration)
explorerhat.motor.one.stop()
```

10
THE ARTS IN STEM: STEAM

HELEN CALDWELL, JEAN EDWARDS AND SWAY GRANTHAM

INTRODUCING STEAM

The arts can enhance different stages of a STEM investigation by adding an additional channel of communication with an audience, which may simply be other members of the class, the wider school community or further afield. At the beginning, the arts might offer an inspirational impetus by being part of the learning trigger or prompt. While work is ongoing, the arts can help to make connections between learners. Towards the end of a project, the arts can engage an audience and communicate results. Seen in this way, explicit art within STEM-based activities can act as bridges to communicate ideas with others. The arts may be enfolded into any part of the learning, as a multimodal channel for learning, a catalyst for ideas, or as a mediation tool that makes the ideas more accessible to others. For example, a product of a STEM investigation may be a data representation that draws upon visual literacy skills to interpret scientific findings. A key question is: what do the arts add to the process of STEM enquiry and vice versa?

IN THIS CHAPTER

This chapter explores the theme of STEM to STEAM, adding the arts to enhance science, technology, engineering and mathematics.

We suggest taking a broad view of the arts to include genres such as science fiction, poetry, dance and performance, graphic novels and installations alongside the more conventional visual arts and music, and recognising ways in which different artistic genres overlap. An additional consideration is that STEAM subjects do not necessarily all have to be present in equal proportions.

To give an example, one primary class investigated how Victorian inventions use light to solve problems and created prototype inventions out of Micro:bits, conductive dough and LEDs. They deconstructed their models and re-represented them as a physical dance performance so that others could guess their inventions. The addition of the arts through the dough modelling linked physical making with the use of digital technology, and the dance provided an additional channel of communication for the children's ideas. Having a collaborative performance or a shareable artefact as an outcome of an activity creates a sense of purpose for a group investigation as children are making something for an audience.

Figure 10.1

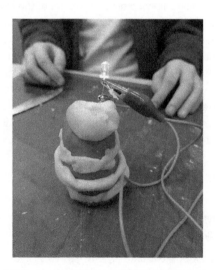

Figure 10.2   Pupils making dough models of Victorian inventions with micro:bits and LEDs

In the context of the primary classroom, STEAM collaborations and exchanges between classes of children can help to build shared understandings and provide an audience for their artistic outputs. A connected classroom approach is something we would encourage you to try. In a local context, exchanges between classes can provide a powerful impetus for learning and making and, in an international context, the addition of the arts can bypass language barriers and build intercultural understandings. In work of this nature, digital technology can become a lens for looking at the world and manipulated media can represent new viewpoints that invite feedback from others.

Such approaches tie in with a growing trend around the world that uses STEAM across educational sectors to create a fertile environment for inquiry-based learning. For example, Connor et al. (2016), in New Zealand, outline five HE engineering student-centric STEAM projects designed to promote active, curious learning; in the US, Radziwill et al. (2015) describe a collaboration on a piece of partici-patory art between science, technology, arts and design students; Land (2013) describes a number of STEAM curricula initiatives developed across the US; and Saddiqui and Marcus (2017) suggest that their STEAMpunk Girls Co-Design program can prompt secondary-aged young women to pursue STEM study and careers in Australia.

One recurring aim across these projects is to mirror the complexity and interconnectedness of work-based professional environments that often combine aspects of STEAM. This helps to prepare students for the challenges of real world problem solving, which often draws upon inductive thinking and the practical application of knowledge to find creative solutions. A second recurring theme across these examples is a view of uncertainty and failure as positive learning opportunities. Art-making is character-ised by risk-taking and playful experimentation; it is acceptable not to have all the answers.

INTRODUCING DESIGN THINKING

A popular approach for problem-based STEAM learning that makes space for creativity alongside the sci-entific process is *design thinking* (Kimbell, 2015). Design thinking begins by empathising with end users and their needs, and puts an emphasis on exploring and defining a key question before framing a problem. It is more akin to problem posing rather than problem solving. A double diamond model can be used to describe divergent and convergent thinking stages that allow for creative discovery phases before making decisions about problems and solutions. Time for creativity is built into a structured approach to solving problems.

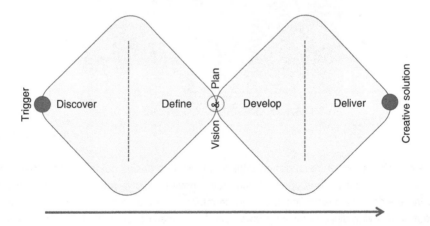

Figure 10.3   Adaptation of the UK Design Council's 'Double Diamond' model (https://www. ebi.ac.uk/training/online/course/user-experience-design/phases-design)

Each diamond combines divergent and convergent thinking, allowing time to explore ideas before refining them. The double diamond indicates that this happens twice; once to discover and define the problem, and secondly to develop and deliver the solution. The process has three key outputs: a trigger, a vision and plan, and a creative solution.

In using this model, the role of the teacher is firstly to present a trigger or impetus to inspire the class to begin thinking creatively. The trigger might be taken from the arts, such as an image, film, sculpture or story. It could be accompanied by a 'what if ...?' question (e.g. What if the world flooded? What if one of our senses changed?).

Next comes an ideation session that gives children time to research and define problems or issues they would like to explore. During this stage, children are encouraged to think 'out of the box' and articulate all their ideas without rejecting any as unfeasible. Teachers often use post-its, or write on the walls, the floor, or the surface of tables to encourage creative thinking. Alternatives are digital tools such as Padlet or Popplet that allow collaborative posting on a virtual wall. At the end of this phase, the ideas can be grouped into themes and children can vote on which they would prefer to take forward. This might be achieved by adding sticky dots to post-its or through an online voting tool such as Socrative.

Figure 10.4 The ideation phase

Once a vision and plan are agreed, design thinking moves into design doing. Children are given time to develop ideas for a creative solution and bring their innovations alive through prototyping and refining ideas during the delivery phase. Again, this phase might include an artistic product or have an artistic aspect to it. In this way, design thinking draws upon logic, imagination and intuition to explore possibilities of what could be, and then communicates outcomes with an audience or end user in mind.

AN EXAMPLE OF A DESIGN THINKING STEAM PROJECT

To draw an example from a recent international project involving classes in four countries, Digital Learning across Boundaries (http://dlaberasmus.eu), children explored the trigger question, what if we moved to space? Excerpts from the trailer for the film *The Martian* (2015) were used to hook and excite the children, together with virtual reality goggles and Google Expeditions. They were invited by NASA to research the idea of a new sustainable planet. Some children exchanged images of their playgrounds, classrooms, sports centre and library to get inspiration for building an ideal school in space. Each class created a different room for the space school and made models and videos to share their solutions. They chose from a variety of materials and techniques, including Lego, woodwork, aerial photography and green screening.

Other pairs of classrooms investigated conditions for survival in space, carried out experiments to produce electricity with solar cells, to produce oxygen by using electrolysis, and programmed robots to search for water. They made model landscapes and recorded videos explaining why their planets were suitable for human survival. Further pairs of classes chose to design and test landing craft and create music based on sounds from their countries.

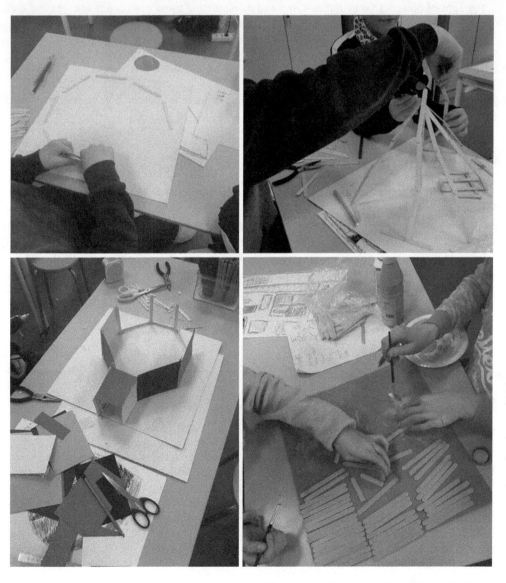

Figure 10.5   Prototyping ideas for a school in space

This project can be analysed using STEAM:

- Science: How conditions such as gravity and atmosphere in space would affect us. Investigating basic requirements for human survival.

- Technology: Using Google SketchUp and bridge construction software to test the strength of structures. Finding images of planets in Google Earth. Building robots with sensors to carry out missions.

- Engineering: Systematically planning and constructing model rooms and writing manuals. Building prototypes for landing on a planet using Paint3D, and then designing and testing them.

- Art: Allowing time to create aesthetically pleasing models out of 'good' materials. Taking aerial photographs of objects to create plan views and manipulating them in a collage app. Making a giant patchwork planet inspired by images from Google Earth. Composing music based on sounds from Earth.

- Mathematics: Making models to scale and experimenting with geometric shapes in 2D and 3D.

A key aspect of all this work was the making of artefacts to share with each other to develop a vision of the developing community in space.

INTRODUCTION TO THE ACTIVITIES

This chapter's three projects promote real world exploration and creative problem solving through physical and digital making. The first project links with the science of light by exploring ways of painting with torches in the dark and capturing the results as photographs. The second project begins with an investigation of the mathematics of snowflake designs and then applies the resulting knowledge of shape and symmetry to printmaking. The focus of the third project is computing: pupils create electrical circuits and program LED lights to add another dimension to their design and technology work and create a piece of flashing art.

ACTIVITY

Painting with Light

What you need to know

Most painting and drawing techniques that children encounter in primary school are based around manipulating tools such as pencils, crayons, pens and paintbrushes to make marks on surfaces such as paper and card. In this activity the use of digital technology allows them to use light (from torches, LED lights and glow sticks) to draw or paint in the dark. An experience that would usually be ephemeral can be captured by the slow shutter app on a tablet or mobile phone. For children being introduced to the science of light in Year 3 or developing their understanding in Year 6 this activity gives them the opportunity to explore using light in a creative context. It also allows them to explore aspects of the computing curriculum.

Preparation

Objective

Create a piece of art using a slow shutter app and sources of light.

Curriculum links

Art and design: using a range of materials creatively; the techniques of drawing, painting or collage; exploration of colour and pattern.

Computing: using, expressing and developing ideas using digital technology.

Science: light.

Year groups

Years 3 (introduction) and 6 (developing understanding).

Equipment

Torches, small LED lights, glow sticks.

Tablets or mobile devices with a slow shutter app.

A dark space to work in.

Useful links

The website of artist Eric Staller, a pioneer of painting with light: http://ericstaller.com/studio-work/light-drawings

Setting the scene

Talk with children about the tools and surfaces we use for drawing or painting. Their ideas will probably focus on the tactile tools and materials with which they are familiar. Show some images of the light drawings of artists Eric Staller and collect other images made with light. Recall writing with sparklers on Bonfire Night.

Show the devices children can use (e.g. torches, LEDs) and explain how digital technology can allow us to paint with light in the dark. Demonstrate how to use the slow shutter app to capture the movement of the lights in one image. Working in pairs is an effective approach for this activity, so that one child uses the device and one moves the lights and then they can swap roles.

Trigger questions

When children are painting with light, they could be challenged to create some specific effects:

- Can you draw a circle?
- Can you write your name?
- Can you make separate marks?
- Can you make continuous lines?

(Continued)

(Continued)

Time to experiment

As children become more independent and confident they can be challenged to experiment and be more creative:

- What can you do with the range of lights available?
- How does moving the lights in different ways change what you can do?
- Can you attach the lights to something to change the way they can be moved?

Review and reflect

Sharing the photographs children have made and discussing how they used the light making tools and the app to create their images is a valuable opportunity for them to demonstrate to each other and share what they have learned.

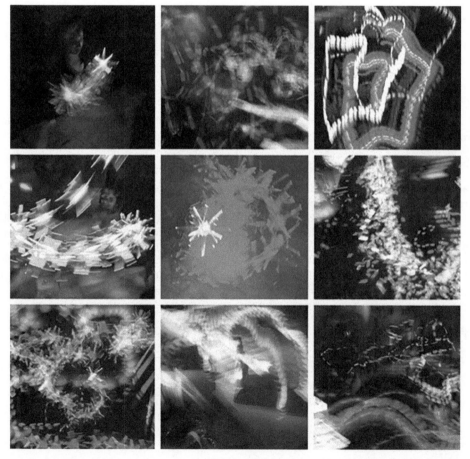

Figure 10.6   Examples of using a slow shutter app

Questioning can draw out discussion about the use of colour, line and pattern in their images. This will help them go beyond playing with light to becoming artists using light as a tool and composing images for viewers to enjoy. Displaying the images on a large screen can be useful. This kind of art is best displayed digitally rather than printed out.

Assessment

It is likely children will create and save a large number of images, so making choices about which to keep and which to delete is a worthwhile activity. This will help them evaluate what they have made. They could be encouraged to consider their images in relation to some prompts:

- How have you used colour in your image?
- How have you used lines, marks and patterns?
- How would you develop or change this image?
- How might you add sound or words to develop this further?

Follow-up activities

Children could use another app to integrate text into their images, e.g. a title, a poem. They could add music and/or sound effects using apps such as Garage Band. The images can be developed further in other art apps by adding drawing or painting, or manipulating the image digitally.

Another approach to exploring light and dark in painting is the use of UV fluorescent paint and UV black light torches.

ACTIVITY

Exploring Snowflakes

What you need to know

Children are usually familiar with folding a circle of paper into sectors, then cutting to create a paper snowflake. When they do this, they usually fold the paper into quarters or eighths. If we take a closer look at magnified images of snowflakes their structure is based on sixths.

Mathematically, folding a circle into sixths can allow children to explore using measurement of angles. Older children can use an angle measurer to divide the 360 degrees of a circle into 60 degree sectors. Younger children who are not ready to learn to use an angle measurer can use a circle with the outline of a clock face instead: two sectors (e.g. from 12 to 2) are one-sixth of the circle. Alternatively, there is a link below to a video demonstration of how to fold a circle into sixths.

A technique that lends itself readily to this activity is printmaking because snowflakes are constructed in six repeating sectors. Children can design and make one of the sectors and then print it

(Continued)

(Continued)

six times to create their complete snowflake. This takes advantage of the inherent feature of many printmaking processes: more than one print can be made leading to exploration of repositioning and repetition.

Preparation

Objectives

To use sixths of a circle to make a repeating pattern.

Curriculum links

Art and design: using a range of materials creatively; the technique of printmaking; exploration of shape and pattern.

Mathematics: properties of shapes; geometry; symmetry; angles; fractions.

Year groups

Years 2 to 4, a clock face can be used with younger children, older children could use an angle measurer (protractor).

Equipment

Scissors, glue, pencils and biros.

Paper: black, white.

Printmaking resources: rollers, trays; white printmaking ink; polystyrene printing tiles.

Access to a photocopier (optional).

Circles to draw around: lids, saucers, plates, card templates.

Clock face template (if working with younger children).

Angle measurers (if working with older children).

Images of magnified snowflakes (see links below).

Useful links

The NOAA photograph library: www.photolib.noaa.gov/nws/newsnowice1.html

Wilson Bentley website: www.snowflakebentley.com

Snowflake resources: www.its.caltech.edu/~atomic/snowcrystals/kids/kids.htm

Digital spirograph: https://nathanfriend.io/inspirograph

Snowflake maker apps: iOS Snow Creator; iOS Happy Snowflake; iOS The Flake Factory.

How to fold into sixths: http://makeitatyourlibrary.org/play/6-pointed-paper-snowflakes#.W5J_l-hKg2x

Setting the scene

Provide children with some images of magnified snowflakes to investigate: these could be printed or presented digitally using resources at the links above. Ask the children to look carefully at the construction of the snowflakes.

Trigger questions

When investigating the images of snowflakes:

- How many sectors are there in each snowflake?
- Can you identify any lines of symmetry?

Time to experiment

Finding one sixth of a circle

To find a sixth of a circle children might use a clock face, an angle measurer or a teacher made template, depending on what would most suit their learning needs.

Designing a pattern

Take the sixth of a circle and fold it in half.

Cut it in different ways. Children should try this out several times experimenting with using different shapes and sizes.

Evaluating the pattern

After children have had time to explore it is useful to lay out all the sectors on a contrasting background to look at the different approaches and learn from each other. This is an opportunity to ask some children to demonstrate how they made some of their patterns. It is useful to draw children's attention to:

- The differences when cuts are made to the folded edge or the edges that open.
- The effect of cutting out sections of different sizes.
- The balance of cutting out too much or too little.
- Where the lines of symmetry are.

The next stage of this activity is to use the sectors to make whole snowflakes. One quick and easy way to do this is to photocopy each of the sectors five times and compile the six sectors into a full snowflake.

Outlined below is a printmaking sequence that gives children much more opportunity to use and develop art skills.

When children have designed a sector that is pleasing to them this can used as a pattern to create a polystyrene tile to print from. Working on a larger scale can be helpful here, especially for younger children.

(Continued)

(Continued)

The paper sector can be placed onto a piece of smooth fine polystyrene. Using a pencil or a biro the 'holes' should be drawn around and then pushed out using the pencil or pen. At this stage, additional small details can be added such as spots and lines although care should be taken to retain the symmetry.

When the polystyrene tile is complete, encourage children to consider:

- Is the pattern symmetrical?
- Is the polystyrene surface sufficiently indented?

The polystyrene tile can now be used for printing the full snowflake:

- Use only small amounts of printing ink on the roller.
- Take care when placing the tile (pencil guidelines can be useful).
- Make sure there is enough time to practise and get better at printing the tile. Both the tile and the printer tend to improve with practice.

Review and reflect

When the print is complete, a repeat of six prints around a point, have a look at the pattern to see how the symmetry design works and consider the use of the printmaking process by looking at the prints.

Encourage children to evaluate their work and talk about what they have learned.

Figure 10.7   The sequence of printing the snowflake pattern using a one sixth piece

Assessment

- Do the edges of each sector line up or are there gaps/overlaps?
- Where is the symmetry in the print?

Follow-up activities

Scientists give names to types of snowflakes: there are 121 names used to describe and classify snowflakes. Children could devise their own name for their snowflake based on its appearance or devise a name with more poetic and imaginative thoughts in mind.

Explore the same ideas in a different context: this activity can be adapted to other objects with symmetrical properties such as six-petalled flowers.

ACTIVITY

Adding LEDs to Art Projects

What you need to know

If children do not already have a secure understanding of a basic circuit, you may wish to spend some time recapping this before the children attempt to connect their LED and program it. The children need to know that we need two wires from the batteries to whatever needs the electricity and that without electricity the device will not work.

If the Crumble controller board has not been used before, it can help to preload a program to make the light turn on. This means that when the children first connect the wires correctly, the light will automatically come on. They can then program it themselves to change the colour of the light.

Children should have previously created a piece of artwork that they wish to add coloured lights to. It is unnecessary to make any holes in the artwork as the lights are bright enough to shine through most materials. The artwork should be designed with the lights in mind but can use whatever artistic principles the children have been working on. Lighter materials such as pencil crayons and watercolours work best because they let through the most light. The subject of the artwork can be adapted to suit the topic of your choice, e.g. stars twinkling in the sky, flashing lights on emergency vehicles, the lava in a volcano.

Preparation

Objectives

To program an LED.

Curriculum links

Computing: design, write and debug programs that accomplish specific goals, including controlling or simulating physical systems; solve problems by decomposing them into smaller parts; use sequence, selection, and repetition in programs; work with variables and various forms of input and output.

(Continued)

(Continued)

Art and design: drawing, painting and sculpture with a range of materials.

Design and technology: understand and use electrical systems in their products; apply their understanding of computing to program, monitor and control their products.

Science: construct a simple series electrical circuit.

Year groups

Years 3 to 6.

Equipment

Crumble Controller Starter Kit.

Piece of artwork.

3 × AA batteries per starter kit.

Laptops with free Crumble software installed.

Useful links

https://redfernelectronics.co.uk/crumble

http://code-it.co.uk/crumble/crumble

Setting the scene

Remind children of the piece of artwork they have already created and how they planned to use the lights to enhance the work. Remind them there is no need to make holes in their existing work as the lights can shine through the paper and will be taped inside/at the back.

Use this time to remind the children of their understanding of circuits. What do we need to light up a bulb? Batteries? Wires? Bulbs? Explain how multi-coloured LEDs need more than just two wires to make the circuit as they need both electricity and 'data' that tells the light what colour to be.

Trigger questions

Why do we need to use batteries in our circuit?

Why are there three wires connected to the LED?

What does this program do?

Can you make the lights flash?

How do you change the colour of the light?

Time to experiment

The children need to wire the battery to their crumble and the LED on the opposite side (note that when using Crumbles the LEDs are called 'Sparkles'). Younger learners might want to copy an existing circuit whereas older learners can figure it out for themselves. For year 6, you could create a simple circuit in a diagram showing how to make the connections and allow them to use this to connect their Crumble. When they have connected it correctly, the light should be the colour of the last program.

Once the children successfully connect the wires to make the circuit their light will come on. Now they need to program the Crumble board with their own code to make it light up as they want. After plugging in the Crumble to their computer, they can use the Crumble software to create simple programs to change the colour of the light and make multiple light sequences.

Attach the lights to the back/inside of the artwork without disturbing the connections to show off their final piece.

Figure 10.8   Adding flashing lights to artwork

Review and reflect

Can you use what you know about circuits to attach another LED to the first one – like a string of fairy lights?

Can you suggest amendments to your original artwork that would make it easier to add the LEDs?

Can you explain how you would use a switch in your circuit? What impact would it have on the LEDs?

Have you added variety to the program? Does it switch colours? Flash on and off? Could you make your program more complex by adding brightness changes?

Assessment

Encourage children to self-assess:

(Continued)

(Continued)

- I can make a circuit using wires and batteries.
- I can design a piece of artwork suitable for adding lights.
- I can create a simple program including a loop.
- I can evaluate my creation and suggest possible improvements.

Follow-up activities

Adding a second light or a switch to the circuit and adapting the program accordingly.

SUMMARY

The activities in this chapter have used physical and digital art as a vehicle for exploring the science of light, the mathematics of shapes and fractions, electrical circuits and computer programming. Art has been a form of inspiration through the light paintings of Eric Staller, and a form of communication as children share snowflake prints and illuminated artworks. The activities illustrate how the creative process can be informed by children's knowledge of science, mathematics and computing. In this chapter, we have presented the model of Design Thinking as a way of adding structure and definition to children's creativity within STEAM investigations and encouraging independent learning.

REFERENCES

Connor, A. M., Karmokar, S. & Whittington, C. (2016) From STEM to STEAM: strategies for enhancing engineering and technology education. *International Journal of Engineering Pedagogy (iJEP)*, 5(2), 37–47.

Kimbell, L. (2015) Rethinking design thinking: part I. *Design and Culture*, 3(3), 285–306.

Land, M. H. (2013) Full STEAM ahead: the benefits of integrating the arts into STEM. *Procedia Computer Science*, 20, 547–552.

Radziwill, N. M., Benton, M. C. & Moellers, C. (2015) From STEM to STEAM: reframing what it means to learn. *The STEAM Journal*, 2(1), 3.

Saddiqui, S. & Marcus, M. (2017) STEAMpunk girls co-design: exploring a more integrated approach to STEM engagement for young women. In *28th Annual Conference of the Australasian Association for Engineering Education (AAEE 2017)*. Barton, ACT: Australasian Association for Engineering Education, p. 1175.

WEBSITES

The Digital Learning across Boundaries project website: http://dlaberasmus.eu

Google Expeditions virtual reality teaching tool: https://itunes.apple.com/us/app/expeditions/id1131711060?mt=8

11

PREPARING FOR TRANSITION TO SECONDARY STEM

DAVID BARLEX

There is little doubt that the government in England sees the STEM (science, technology, engineering and mathematics) subjects as being important to the economy. There have been a series of government reports since 2000 arguing for greater emphasis on the STEM subjects culminating in a National STEM Programme (DFES and DTI, 2006). One of the difficulties noted by John Holman, the National Director of the Programme, was the disparity in status of the STEM subjects in school. He summed this up well with the following graphic device:

In school:

$S_{TE}M$

In the world outside school:

$_S TE_M$

John argued that there should be a better balance across the STEM subjects in school. This disparity of status is reinforced by school accountability measures. At the end of Key Stages 1 and 2, only mathematics is the focus of high stakes testing. Science is tested by national sample every two years at the end of Key Stage 2. At age 16, the English Baccalaureate (EBacc) performance measure requires students to obtain GCSE grade C or better (grade 5 from 2017/18) in English, mathematics, two sciences, history or geography (referred to as humanities), and an ancient or modern foreign language. The T and the E are notable only by their absence. Refining John's graphic:

In primary school:

$S_{TE}M$

In secondary school:

$S_{TE}M$

In the world beyond school, STEM specialists work together in multi-disciplinary teams. In many schools planning and teaching does not exploit the natural links between STEM subjects, resulting in S.T.E.M, the full stops between the initials illustrating the lack of interaction. When barriers are overcome we can legitimately write the acronym as STEM and teachers can 'look sideways in the curriculum' and teach in the light of STEM. So, the teaching of one STEM subject is informed by the learning that has already taken place in other STEM subjects to the benefit of all these subjects. For example, a design and technology topic would make explicit use of mathematics and science that had already been taught. This would enhance learning in all three aspects of the curriculum. In secondary school, with different teachers teaching design and technology, science and mathematics it can be difficult to show improvements in learning across the three subjects. However, in primary school the same teacher is usually responsible for teaching all three subjects so it is easier for the teacher to find evidence of enhanced learning in all subjects. Also, the primary teacher can plan work so that the 'looking sideways' can require the use of knowledge and skills from one subject as it has been taught.

MAKING THE MOST OF THE TRANSITION EXPERIENCE

A key feature of this transition experience is 'a visit' in which primary school children visit their intended secondary school with examples of STEM work. Clearly such visits will require some orchestration to be successful. Prior to the visit, it will be important for the primary school to discuss with the secondary school the nature of the work that the children will be bringing on the visit. The work could be discussed well in advance so that the secondary school might, if it is appropriate, make some suggestions. Whether this can take place or not, it is important that the secondary schools know about the work the children have undertaken. Meeting the children with their work will give the secondary school teachers real insight into the achievements of the primary children and reveal the extent to which the STEM subjects have been able to collaborate in the primary school. And the secondary school teachers will be able to organise the visit so they provide experiences and activities that consolidate and extend the learning that has taken place as well as introducing the children to some of the teachers and the facilities in the mathematics, science, and design and technology departments.

Such transition experiences will benefit the three key stakeholders. The secondary school teachers will understand the learning that has taken place in the primary school and be in a stronger position to build on this. The primary school teacher will see where their teaching leads and be able to tailor their teaching to support transition. The children will see that their work is valued by both the primary school and the secondary school and realise that their learning will have continuity.

ACTIVITY

Starting with Mathematics: Creating Creatures

What you need to know

Taking the study of 'properties of shape' as the starting point, children will use their knowledge and understanding of polygons to design and make creatures living on the imaginary world Geomiter where creatures are constructed from geometric shapes. They will also think about their possible life cycles and habitats.

This work will be followed by a transition experience in which children take some of the creatures with details of their possible life cycles and habitats with them when they visit the secondary school towards the end of primary school. These learning outcomes will form the starting point of the transition experience. The secondary school teachers can talk with children about what they have done and work with them on how they can extend this learning.

The children's activity is to envisage an imaginary world (Geomiter) in which the living things are made from geometric shapes and to design a range of creatures using their knowledge and understanding of polygons that can be slotted together as the starting point for the activity. Children will be able to use their knowledge and understanding of the nature and classification of living things, habitats and life cycles to write encyclopaedia entries describing life on planet Geomiter.

Preparation

Objectives

To create a creature using interlocking geometric shapes.

To consider the habitat and lifecycle of their creature.

To prepare an encyclopaedia entry for their creature.

Curriculum links

Mathematics: construction of triangles, rectangles and simple polygons using their properties.

Science: the nature of living things and their habitats, their life cycles and their classification into broad groups.

Design and technology: how to join sheet materials together using slots; how to reinforce structures; design, make, evaluate.

English: writing for a specific audience.

Year groups

Aimed primarily at Year 6, with a view to supporting primary–secondary school transition.

Equipment

Plain paper, thin card, thick card, corrugated card, graph paper, pairs of compasses, rulers, pencils, scissors, digital cameras and computers.

Useful links

The Life Collection of David Attenborough TV programmes available at www.amazon.co.uk/ Attenborough-Life-Collection-Sir-David/dp/B00MCKN7RO/ref=sr_1_2?s=dvdandie=UTF8andqid= 1466419059andsr=1-2andkeywords=david+attenborough will provide a tremendous stimulus and resource for imagining life on Geomiter.

(Continued)

(Continued)

Setting the scene

Begin by discussing the idea of transition to secondary school and suggest that children can share their work from this project with their new teachers, demonstrating their work in mathematics, science and design and technology.

Introduce the planet Geomiter that is much like planet Earth in many ways, with similar weather, seas and oceans and continents. But, there is one important difference. The animals and plants that live on Geomiter are made up of polygons, joined together through slots. Tell the class they will be designing and making a creature that lives on Geomiter. They will begin by developing their work on properties of shape as they will be using shapes of various sorts to create creatures that live on the imaginary world of Geomiter.

It would be useful to show the class how a simple animal form body, head and four legs can be made up from simple rectangles slotted together as shown in the illustration below.

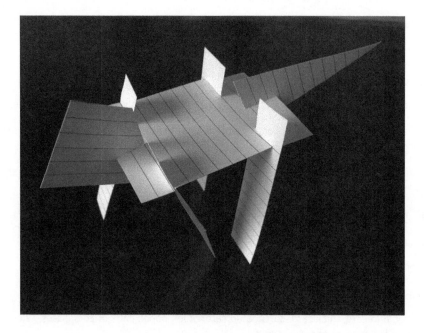

Tell the children they must decide what the creatures might look like and how they live and behave in their various habitats. They will describe this in an encyclopaedia entry they write about the creature they create.

Show the class an example encyclopaedia entry for an animal that exists on earth, like the example below (taken from Wikipedia).

One species of African elephant, the bush elephant (*Loxodonta africana*), is the largest living terrestrial animal, while the forest elephant (*Loxodonta cyclotis*) is the third largest. Their thick-set bodies rest on stocky legs, and they have concave backs. Their large ears enable heat loss. The upper lip and nose form a trunk. The trunk acts as a fifth limb, a sound amplifier, and an important method of touch. African elephants' trunks end in two opposing lips, whereas the Asian elephant trunk ends in a single lip. In *L. africana*, males stand 3.2–4.0 m (10–13 ft) tall at the shoulder and weigh 4,700–6,048 kg (10,360–13,330 lb), while females stand 2.2–2.6 m (7–9 ft) tall and weigh 2,160–3,232 kg (4,762–7,125 lb); *L. cyclotis* is smaller with male shoulder heights of up to 2.5 m (8 ft). The largest recorded individual stood four metres (13.1 ft) at the shoulders and weighed 10 tonnes.

Explain to the children that this activity is an opportunity to revisit some of their science learning about living things and their habitats as well as extending their mathematics learning about the properties of shapes in a design and technology activity. This will help to improve their learning in science, mathematics, and design and technology.

They will take the creatures they design and make and their encyclopaedia entries with them on the 'transition visit' to the secondary school to show the teachers there what they have been learning and the sort of work they have been doing.

Trigger questions

- What do we mean by habitat? Give an example.
- What do we mean by lifecycle? Give an example.
- What are the names for three-, four-, five- and six-sided polygons?
- What does having parallel sides mean? Give an example.
- Explain the difference between a regular and irregular polygon.
- Explain the differences between an amphibian, a reptile, a bird and a mammal.
- What is the difference between predator and prey? Give an example.
- What needs to be included in an encyclopaedia entry?

(Continued)

(Continued)

Time to experiment

Children can work individually or in pairs.

Construct a variety of polygons (e.g. isosceles triangles, equilateral triangles, squares, rectangles, parallelograms, regular and irregular pentagons, regular and irregular hexagons) on paper, cut them out and experiment with putting slots in the shapes and joining them together.

Decide on the polygons to use for their creature – construct templates for the polygons on paper.

Use the templates to produce the polygons in stiff or corrugated card.

Experiment with assembling the 3D structure of their creature – at this stage, children may need to modify their design to ensure stability and refine sizing etc.

Research possible habitat and life cycle for their creature.

Write the encyclopaedia entry for their creature.

Review and reflect

There are four key points where children can check their progress through the activity: viability of creature design, feasibility of habitat and lifecycle, construction of the creature and the encyclopaedia entry. At each stage, children should be encouraged to consider what is going well, what they might want to change and where they might need help.

Create a classroom display of the creatures and encyclopaedia entries and provide a time when children can discuss with one another what they created and why. When the activity is complete, children should ask themselves the following questions:

- What did I enjoy most?
- What did I enjoy the least?
- What did I find easy?
- What did I find difficult?
- What did I get better at?
- What did I do to help others in the class?
- What did others in the class do to help me?
- What might I have been done better? How?

Children should use their reflections to answer the following important transition question:

What will I tell the secondary school teachers about my STEM learning when I show them the creature I have designed and made and the encyclopaedia entry that describes the way it lives?

Assessment

Through observation of children's work, it will be possible to find out how confident children are with the mathematics, science, design and technology and English knowledge and skills relevant to the classroom. For peer assessment, the children can evaluate each other's creature and encyclopaedia entry. They might ask each other:

- About properties of polygons

  o   What did you learn about polygons from designing your creature?

- About construction

  o   What did you learn about joining shapes together by means of slots?

- About living things and their habitats

  o   What did you learn about life cycles and habitats by producing the encyclopaedia entry?

Follow-up activities

Children could extend their work to consider other life forms on Geomiter. They could produce a food web for the various life forms showing how they depend on one another. This could become an additional encyclopaedia entry.

ACTIVITY

Starting with Science: Falling but Slowly

What you need to know

Taking 'exploring and explaining forces' as a starting point, children will investigate the performance of simple parachutes and use the results to inform designing and making simple parachute toys for particular users. They will also need to use nets and accurate measuring to produce toys that are fit for purpose.

This work will be followed by a transition experience in which children take details of their investigations and some of the parachute toys with them when they visit the secondary school towards the end of primary school. These learning outcomes will form the starting point of the transition experience. The secondary school teachers can talk with children about what they have done and work with them on how they can extend this learning.

(Continued)

(Continued)

The activity includes investigating the performance of different, simple parachute designs and using the results of the investigation to design and make simple parachute toys. The parachute canopies will be made from single sheets of tissue paper cut, folded and joined to produce a variety of 3D forms from nets, including cones. Children will be able to investigate the effect of form and the number of attachments (made from cotton thread) on the speed of falling and the stability of the chute. The toys might be simple 'throw as high as you can and enjoy the descent' or a chute for a small toy figure, e.g. a Lego person. Larger toy figures might require several chutes that would complicate the design as it would be important for the multiple chutes not to interfere with one another.

Preparation

Objectives

To design a toy that uses parachute(s) to impede the rate of falling.

Curriculum links

Science: force, in particular the effect of gravity causing bodies to fall towards the Earth and the effects of air resistance including the possibility of instability during falling; fair testing and related experimental procedures.

Design and technology: cut and join different materials (e.g. cotton thread, tissue paper and card); design, make and evaluate.

Mathematics: design of nets that could be used as forms for parachutes.

Year groups

Aimed primarily at Year 6, with a view to supporting primary–secondary school transition.

Equipment

Tissue paper, graph paper, card, pairs of compasses, rulers, scissors, PVA glue, cotton thread, string, timing devices, tape measures, objects for use with parachutes including toy figures, device for video recording.

Useful links

Toys from Trash: www.arvindguptatoys.com/toys-from-trash.php www.arvindguptatoys.com/toys/Polytheneparachute.html

Setting the scene

Tell the children they will be thinking about the work they did on 'forces' and 'how science works' to investigate what makes a good parachute.

Explain they will use the results of their investigation to design a parachute toy. The sort of parachute toy they design is up to them but it might be a simple 'throw and enjoy' toy, a chute for a small toy figure or a chute for a larger toy.

They can use tissue paper for the parachute canopies that they can cut, fold and join to give a variety of 3D forms.

Explain how this activity is an opportunity to revisit their science and mathematics learning and use it in a design and technology activity. This will help their learning in science, mathematics, and design and technology.

They will take the parachutes they design and make with them on the 'transition visit' to the secondary school to show the teachers what they have been learning and the sort of work they have been doing.

Trigger questions

- Why do things fall towards the Earth?
- How might we investigate this falling towards the Earth?
- How can the rate of falling be slowed down?
- What shape of canopy is likely to be best for slowing down a fall?
- What factors might affect how well a canopy works?
- How can the canopy be attached?
- What is the effect of a hole in the canopy?

Time to experiment

Children can carry out the following activities in pairs.

Make simple parachutes and compare their performance.

Investigate the effect of using objects of different mass.

Adapt the plans to improve performance.

Investigate the effect of including holes of different sizes and in different places in the canopy.

Investigate how the use of different size and shape toys affects the performance of the parachute.

Design their parachute toy, justifying the choices they make.

Review and reflect

There are four staging points where children can check their progress through the activity. These are:

(Continued)

(Continued)

1. When they have investigated the size and shape of the net for the parachute - how does the size and shape of the net affect the way the parachute falls?

2. When they have investigated the effect of a central hole on the way a parachute falls - how does a central hole in the canopy affect the way the parachute falls?

3. When they have investigated how different sized and shaped toys affect the way the parachute falls - how does the toy affect the way the parachute falls?

4. When they have designed a harness to hold their toy to the parachute - how does the parachute perform?

When these reflections are complete the children should ask themselves the following questions:

- What did I enjoy most?
- What did I enjoy the least?
- What did I find easy?
- What did I find difficult?
- What did I get better at?
- What did I do to help others in the class?
- What did others in the class do to help me?
- What could I have done better? How?

Children should use these reflections to answer the following important transition question:

What will I tell the secondary school teachers about my STEM learning when I tell them about my investigations into parachutes and show them the parachute toy I have designed and made?

Assessment

For peer to peer assessment the children can jointly evaluate the investigations they carried out and how they used the results. They might ask each other:

- About their investigations
  - What did I learn from my investigations about the shape and size of net that makes a good parachute?
  - What did I learn from my investigations about the effect of a central hole on the way a parachute falls?
  - What did I learn about the effect of different size and shape toys on the way a parachute falls?

- About using their results
  - How did I use these findings in the design of my parachute toy?

For your assessment of their science learning you can use their peer to peer assessment, the contents of their science investigation notebook, the parachute toy itself and any observations you made during the lessons to assess their science investigation skills and understanding of forces.

Follow-up activities

Children can devise additional games to be played with the parachute toys that involve getting the parachute to land in a particular place from a variety of different jumping off points in different 'windy' conditions provided by a hair dryer. In response to these games they can devise investigations to identify changes to the parachute design that improves performance.

ACTIVITY

Starting with Design and Technology: What Sort of Light Will Work for You?

What you need to know

Taking the designing and making of a lighting device as a starting point the children will need to use their understanding of simple circuits with switches, bulbs and reflective materials (from science) to produce a useful, controllable lighting circuit, and nets to provide an enclosure (from mathematics). This work will be followed by a transition experience in which children take the lighting device plus their circuit diagrams with them when they visit the secondary school during Year 6. These learning outcomes will form the starting point of the transition experience. The secondary school teachers can talk with children about what they have done and work with them on how they can extend this learning.

The activity is to design and make a light that is suitable for use in a particular situation. The device will be constructed mainly from card and technical components but children will be able to use found materials as well. It will be powered by a battery and controlled by switches.

Preparation

Objectives

To design a light for a specific purpose.

To use a circuit diagram for their light.

Curriculum links

Design and technology: how to construct series circuits; how to organise circuits to fit into enclosures; how to arrange switches so they are easy to use.

(Continued)

(Continued)

Science: series circuits with one, two or three batteries and one, two and three bulbs; explain the brightness of the bulbs in different circuits; the role of a switch in a series circuit; how to draw a circuit diagram of a series circuit.

Mathematics: design and construct nets that can be used as enclosures for circuits and batteries.

Year groups

Aimed primarily at Year 6, with a view to supporting primary–secondary school transition.

Equipment

Bulbs and bulb holders, thin insulated wire, thin insulated wire with crocodile clips at either end, paper, batteries, paperclips and paper fasteners, pliers and/or wire cutters/strippers, small screwdrivers, rulers, card, graph paper, rulers, scissors, PVA glue, double-sided and single-sided adhesive tape; aluminium cooking foil for conductors and reflectors, overhead projector film for lenses, tracing paper for light shades, thin wooden strip for frames, coloured paper and coloured stickers for decorations, string to improve grip, straws and small buttons to create texture.

Useful links

A more extensive treatment of this activity can be found in the Nuffield Primary Solutions Unit, 'Which sort of light will work for you?': https://dandtfordandt.files.wordpress.com/2013/01/torchy6.pdf

Setting the scene

Tell the children their activity is to design and make a light suitable for use in a particular situation. Explain they will be using light bulbs for the light source and batteries to power the light bulbs. They will have card to make an enclosure for the circuit. They will have to make the switches that turn the light on and off. They will have to think about who the light is for and where it will be used, as this will affect what the light looks like and how it works. This activity is an opportunity for children to revisit some of their mathematics and science learning and use it in their design and technology learning. As a result, their design and technology learning will be better and they will be able to further develop their understanding of mathematics and science. They will take the lights they design and make with them on the 'transition visit' to the secondary school to show the teachers there what they have been learning and the sort of work they have been doing.

Trigger questions

You can use questions to help children recall science, mathematics and design and technology that are relevant to this activity. You might ask:

- Can anyone explain how I can use these wires and this battery to make this bulb light up?
- Can anyone explain how I can turn this flat piece of card into a cube?
- Can anyone suggest how I might use the cube and the circuit to create a light?

Depending on the answers you receive you can direct children to some small activities that will support their recall and consolidate their learning. These are listed in the next section.

Time to experiment

Children can carry out the following activities in pairs.

Use the batteries, bulbs and wires to light as many bulbs as you can.

Use the batteries, wires and one bulb to get a bulb to shine brightly.

Use card and aluminium foil to make a switch.

Use card, paper fasteners and paperclips to make a switch.

Use card to make a net that folds up into a cube.

Review and reflect

There are four staging points where children can check their progress through the activity. These are:

1. When they have finished constructing the circuit – does the bulb(s) light, does the switch work?
2. When they have finished constructing the net for the enclosure – does it fold up to give the desired shape?
3. When they have finished placing the circuit in the enclosure – does it fit, does the bulb still light, does the switch still work?
4. When they have finished applying any surface embellishments to the net - do they improve the appearance, do they make it easier to use?

When these reflections are complete the children should ask themselves the following questions:

- What did I enjoy most?
- What did I enjoy the least?
- What did I find easy?
- What did I find difficult?

(Continued)

(Continued)

- What did I get better at?
- What did I do to help others in the class?
- What did others in the class do to help me?
- What could I have done better? How?

Children should use these reflections to answer the following important transition question:

What will I tell the secondary school teachers about my STEM learning when I show them the lighting device I have designed and made?

Assessment

For peer to peer assessment the children can jointly evaluate the performance of the lighting devices that they have each designed and made. They might ask each other:

- How well does the light work?

  o Does it give a bright light?
  o Is it easy to switch on and off?
  o Is it easy to change the bulb(s) and the battery?

- How good does the light look?

  o Are there decorations on the light?
  o Do they make it look attractive?

- How well made is the light?

  o Does the enclosure have crisp folds and even surfaces?
  o Do the joins hold together well?

For your assessment of their design and technology learning you can use their peer to peer assessment, the lighting device itself, the contents of their design and technology notebook and any observations you made during the lessons to assess their designing, making, evaluation and technical knowledge and understanding.

Follow-up activities

Children can develop their lighting devices by trying to achieve more brightness or variable brightness. This will involve using parallel circuits with multiple switches.

DISCUSSION: LOOKING SIDEWAYS TO ACHIEVE STEM

This chapter has considered some teaching in each of mathematics, science, and design and technology that might take place at the end of primary school. We have explored how 'looking sideways' might influence the teaching and learning and the transition of children from primary to secondary school. The activities aimed to give each of the subjects equal status in response to John Holman's concern about some STEM subjects having more prestige than others. It is important to consider the following stakeholders and what they might gain from the transition experience: children undergoing transition, primary teachers and secondary teachers.

Planning these joint STEM experiences is important for the primary teacher because it requires becoming familiar with the learning in one subject in the light of its applicability in another. This can often give new insights into the learning taking place in each subject and help to develop a clearer understanding of the nature of that learning for children. Children have the opportunity to appreciate the relevance of mathematics and science when it is used in a design and technology project. When teachers discuss STEM projects across the primary/secondary transition boundary, secondary teachers gain insight into the learning achievements of children in the primary school. The knowledge, skills, understanding and values developed through the transition activities described in this chapter may become lost if children are not encouraged to use them in secondary school.

An important attitude for all learners is their understanding of how they learn and an appreciation of what it means to be a good learner. Good learners do not necessarily find learning easy but they do persevere in the face of difficulties. They do not give up when they find an activity demanding or challenging. Such understanding and perseverance, sometimes called resilience, will stand primary school children in good stead when they reach secondary school and developing these personal qualities is a key feature of the transition projects described here. Through both the nature of the activities themselves (they are deliberately demanding) and the nature of the reviewing and reflection carried out during and at the end of the activities the children learn to persevere and understand how they learn.

REFERENCE

DFES and DTI (2006) *The Science, Technology, Engineering and Mathematics (STEM) Programme Report.* London: DFES.

FURTHER READING

The Connecting STEM Teachers Project led by Dominic Nolan at the Royal Academy of Engineering (see www.raeng.org.uk/education/schools/education-programmes-list/connecting-stem-teachers) has developed a nationwide network of secondary schools in which teachers of the different STEM subjects collaborate. It is very likely that such schools would be very interested in STEM developments in their feeder primary schools and highly supportive of the transition experiences described above.

INDEX